trotman

Music
Industry

UNCOVERED

trotman

Music Industry
UNCOVERED

Tania Shillam

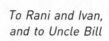

To Rani and Ivan,
and to Uncle Bill

Music Industry Uncovered
This first edition published in 2004 by Trotman and Company Ltd
2 The Green, Richmond, Surrey TW9 1PL

© Trotman and Company Limited 2004

Editorial and Publishing Team

Author Tania Shillam
Editorial Mina Patria, Editorial Director; Rachel Lockhart,
Commissioning Editor; Anya Wilson, Editor;
Bianca Knights, Assistant Editor
Production Ken Ruskin, Head of Pre-press and Production
Sales and Marketing Deborah Jones,
Head of Sales and Marketing
Advertising Tom Lee, Commercial Director
Managing Director Toby Trotman

Designed by XAB

British Library Cataloguing in Publication Data
A catalogue record for this book is available
from the British Library

ISBN 0 85660 965 X

Typeset by Palimpsest Book Production Limited,
Polmont, Stirlingshire

Printed and bound in Great Britain by
Cromwell Press, Trowbridge, Wiltshire

CONTENTS

About the Author

I love writing career advice. I've watched people's eyes sparkle as they remember their attempts to break into their area of the music industry and try to convey that excitement to the reader through my writing. I hope I've done them justice.

My own musical credentials are modest. I play the violin for an amateur orchestra and, in my dreams, I play a red electric violin for a Middle Eastern band. Also, in my dreams, I produce, with some deft editing, my version of 'Love is a Rebellious Bird' from *Carmen* over a house mix. Luckily I wake up and have a day job.

Acknowledgements

I'm very privileged and grateful for the help of: Mina Patria of Trotman Publishing, my colleague at BBC Radio 4 Allan Murray, producer Ahmad Dayes, Moshik and his band Moshikop, Neil Ward-Dutton and his band Clear, Neil Gardener of the Gateway School of Recording and Music Technology, Andrea Terrano of Iguana Studios, Alice Schofield at Anglo Plugging, Ludes manager Sam Elderidge, DJ NIKKI (beatniktv.com – sky digital 184), Momo's DJ Simon, Laure Malca, Music Director for Momo's, Larmer Tree Festival Co-Director Julia Safe, radio producer Jez Broster, and, for completing my book with her inspiring story, Jentina.

Why read this book?

The music industry makes money by the truckload! It is a place where very sharp, talented people congregate. It is also a monster of greed and the pitfalls are plentiful, which we will explore later. If you want to join this industry then you need to focus on the priorities of the monster and keep up to date with the changes that are taking place.

You may know someone in the industry. You may be a complete outsider. Either way, you'll be able to use this book to plan your line of attack and to get to know the structures and complexities of the 'biz'. If you have ambition and tenacity you will make it. As with entering any competitive industry, read and research everything. Inform yourself. Make sure you know what you're letting yourself in for. Make sure that when the knocks come, you have options. Guard against being a one-trick wonder.

FASCINATING FACT

The music industry in the UK is actually quite small and only employs around 122,000 people, according to the British Phonographic Industry (BPI).

Plenty of people are leaving the business because traditional roles are being squeezed out. Affordable music-making technology and the Internet have really rocked the boat. This means that new roles are materialising elsewhere. We need to figure out where.

In pursuit of this, you'll find in these pages an evaluation of:

● the record company structure

● the music-making process and the jobs involved

● where to find work experience placements

● job profiles to give you a taster of the variety of jobs

● the 'brave new world'.

At the moment we are straddling the old traditional world and the new Internet one and there are a myriad of different jobs. I've outlined a few of those jobs but, of course, this represents a fraction of the jobs on offer. There are also tasks for you – conduct your own research and interview your own choice of music industry person.

Trivial pursuit questions:

● What's the difference between an agent and an artist manager?

● What's the difference between 'marketing and promoting' and plugging and being a press officer?

● What's the difference between A&R and talent scout?

● What's the A&R in a publishing house?

● Why is publishing important?

● Exactly how many people take a cut of the artist's earnings?

Answers: Find them in this book and use the Internet!

WHAT WILL YOU GET
FROM THIS BOOK?

If you are looking for a career in mainstream music you will find a better understanding of:

● the role you are going for

● how to get onto the first rung of the ladder

● the people and professions that surround you

● how all the professions fit together to produce the finished, sellable product.

In this book you'll find interviews with professionals that will help you on your way. The advice given is their advice.

They will show you the steps to take and give examples of work. Their experiences will highlight the good and the bad. There are examples, tips and anecdotes that will give you a clear idea of what to do next as well as open your mind up to extra possibilities.

For example, a piece of music needs a targeted audience; a CD needs production; a finished product needs a marketing strategy.

CLASSICAL, JAZZ AND BLUES
Classical, jazz and blues are specialised areas, and I won't be focusing particularly on them but there are areas where knowledge gleaned here can be applied elsewhere. See pages 66–67 for more information.

WHY MUSIC?

First of all, think about why you want a career in the music industry. Be clear about this because it is an industry full of people who think about and talk about very little other than music, fashions, trends and images. To call the majority of them obsessive may be a little strong but it's not far from the truth. People really do live for their music. The question is: Do you?

What is your involvement in music now? Do you find your entertainment in seeking out unsigned bands in pubs and clubs? Do you look for possibilities and new trends? Where do you find your inspiration? Where do you get your buzz? You need to enter your chosen career with passion.

WHY YOU?
Write a paragraph about why you would like to pursue this career. Refine it as you work your way through the book. At some point a potential employer will ask you to justify your application and you must be prepared for this question. You should anticipate such questions and have the answers ready. If you say that you *think* you might be good at 'such-and-such' and that you *think* you might like doing 'so-and-so', faces will fall, big sighs will be heard and you'll be shown the door.

Where do you see yourself? What images do you conjure up when you think of the British music industry? Do you think of vinyl or CDs? Does it make you think of live music, TV entertainment or Internet streaming? Where do you get your music from: on the high street or online? What's your instrument: old-fashioned instrument or new-fangled turntables and PC? Do you picture performers in their 'bling' or chief executives in their suits? Do you picture yourself in a studio, office or venue?

As you work your way through this book, think about where your passion lies. Don't end up in the boardroom if you really belong with a band on the road! On the other hand, if you're offered work experience by your school at the opposite end of the industry to the place you want to end up, it can only be a good thing. Get as broad an understanding as possible.

Think about your career strategy. Should you do work experience in a marketing department if you really want to be in the studio? Well, see the interview with Andrea Terrano (page 30) and his experience of setting up his own studio. He has a service on offer that now needs to be marketed. What about going into finance and accounting if you've barely got your Maths GCSE? Well, take a look at the interview with Neil Ward-Dutton and see how his band financed its own CD production (page 21).

CHAPTER 1

Preparation

INFORM YOURSELF: MUSIC PRESS AND MAINSTREAM PRESS

Keep a notebook and keep ahead of what's happening. You must try to develop your own overview of the industry. Develop your opinions about the changes taking place. Chapter 6, 'Brave New World' will explore this in some detail but make sure you keep up with the news.

Read everything. Familiarise yourself with the music press, for example *NME*, *Q* and *Music Week*. *MAD*, a marketing magazine, explains how hard it is for music magazines to survive, given the volatile nature of the music market:

> '*Uncut* surged ahead in the latest round of ABC's with a 22 per cent year-on-year rise in sales to 111,167, while *Mojo* saw a more modest increase of four per cent to 104,437. Those titles targeted towards younger readers saw a decline, with *NME* falling by 1.1 per cent to 72,557 while *Kerrang* saw a drop of 14,912 copies, representing an 18 per cent slide. *Mixmag* saw a 16 per cent fall to average sales of only 50,182. *Q* managed to remain market leader, despite a fall in sales of over ten per cent year-on-year to 161,634.'
> From *MAD: Hitting The Right Note*, 19 February 2004, (www.mad.co.uk/abc03h2/story.aspx)

Here is a taster of the music magazines, journals and online sites you should take a look at:

Q (www.q4music.com)

Q was launched in October 1986. It calls itself 'the UK's best-selling serious music publication and the first choice for big-name interviews.' It has, of course, music news and reviews. The website has a 'history' page in which it describes that its goal has always been to 'raise the game of music journalism'.

NEW MUSICAL EXPRESS (NME) (www.nme.com)

NME is a premier British music weekly. It is essential reading and has a very proud history. It's been the training ground of many famous celebrity journalists, especially those from the punk era such as Tony Parsons, Julie Burchill as well as DJ Steve Lamacq and radio presenter Danny Kelly. Since the beginnings of rock 'n' roll and every emergent trend since then, it has served its readership with the writings of journalists who have been proud of their craft and very passionate about their music. This is the one to get your head around if you're interested in music journalism.

MOJO (www.mojo4music.com)

An authoritative resource and entertaining all-round music magazine with a great website.

SMASH HITS (www.smashhits.net)

A young, funky, cool, colourful pop magazine.

UNCUT (www.uncut.net)

This is what the publisher (IPC Media) says about the magazine:

'A must for the serious music fan, *Uncut* looks at both classic artists that have stood the test of time along with new musicians and underground trends worth notice. (The) magazine features consistently strong writing, hundreds of music and movie reviews, interviews, news, and a complimentary compilation CD with each issue.'

KERRANG! (www.kerrang.com)
Born in 1981, it calls itself 'the world's biggest selling weekly rock magazine'. It also states: '*Kerrang!* is a TV station, an awards ceremony, the co-promoter of the annual K-Fest gigs, and now a website.'

MUSIC TANK (www.musictank.co.uk)
It calls itself 'the UK's music business network' – take a look. It aims 'to give artists, managers, labels, publishers, promoters, audio professionals, press and beyond the connectivity to share ideas, exchange information and forge new partnerships – whatever the genre'. There's all kinds of information to be found here including web pages for 'Industry Facts and Figures' and 'Training and Education'.

Do some research. Find other magazines, seek out their websites, find the ones that suit you the most while you make sure that you keep abreast of the ones that you're not so in tune with.

Don't ignore the mainstream press. Here's an example of some cuttings I've taken in a matter of days from mainstream news sources:

1) 17 January 2004: The *Guardian* interview with Alan Giles, chief executive of the HMV Group where he talks about when and how HMV will invest in digital delivery. Giles was a physics graduate, before becoming a trainee buyer for Boots. He had no involvement or ambition in the music industry till half a dozen other jobs passed him by.

2) 23 January 2004: The *Evening Standard* profile of Brit band Franz Ferdinand whose second single outsold Beyoncé and Liberty X.

3) 29 January 2004: The *Evening Standard* profile of Katie Melua who sold more than 350,000 albums, has a five-album deal worth £2 million and is 19 years old.

The *Guardian* media web page has a section on the music industry so get into the habit of checking the latest developments: http://media.guardian.co.uk.

Finally the BBC Radio 1 'One Life' website gives career advice.
(From the Radio 1 page click on 'One Life' on the left hand side of
the screen. There's also a 'Music News' link there, and a link to
'1xtra' which has loads of news about Hip Hop, R&B, Garage and
other genres not served by the magazines and newspapers
mentioned above.)

CAREER STRATEGY

Do some research into yourself. Think about what you like, what
you are good at and what interests you.

WHAT DO YOU WANT MOST FROM WORK? CHOOSE YOUR TOP TEN FROM THE LIST BELOW:

To be creative
To be respected
To be fulfilled
To be successful
To be secure
To run on high stress levels
To be effective
To have lots of entertainment
To earn big money
To be an inspiring boss
To be a valuable team player
To be independent
To be acknowledged
To be famous
To find a mentor
To travel
To find a partner
To work abroad
To develop a portfolio career
  (see below)
To have a structured
  workplace

To have a structured day
To have an unstructured
  work life
To have a full-to-bursting
  diary
To take enviable holidays
To be inspired
To be dedicated and
  committed
To find spiritual fulfilment
To have a kickin' social life
To be a troubleshooter
To have health and fitness
To achieve something
  every day
To be left alone
To have access to training
  courses
To fit in children and
  family life

NB: A portfolio career is one where rather than working for
one company, you take on various projects and cultivate
several clients.

CONCLUSION

1) SELF ASSESSMENT

Take time to achieve a greater personal understanding of yourself. This will save you from wasting time in the wrong job. You must learn to assess: whether you're in the wrong job; whether your skills and ambitions are being catered for or not; whether you're just treading water or making progress. If you're not happy, do something about it.

2) MATCH YOUR SKILLS TO THE JOB

Take responsibility. There's a difference between falling helplessly into mediocre job after mediocre job and putting some thought into your moves and their outcomes and ultimately your fulfilment. Make a game plan. Determine your best skills, medium talents, and smallest abilities and chart your goal.

RECOMMENDED READING

Look at another book published by Trotman, *Winning CVs for First-time Job Hunters*, by Kathleen Houston, a working career adviser. It has examples of CVs, advice about content, length and the best font to use and there's a quiz to prepare you to start writing your CV.

Kathleen Houston says that the basis of a compelling CV is:

'Your three strongest and best personality qualities; your strongest and best skills, with examples to prove them; and your experience in any work environment or your key transferable skills.'

Having established these building blocks, she helps you build the 'template CV' and covering letter.

Take a look at books about planning career strategies, creating CVs, writing applications, as this is a very important stage to get right from the start.

CHAPTER 2

Structure of the industry

RECORD COMPANIES AND THEIR DEPARTMENTS

Global market share figures for 2002			
BMG	11.1%	EMI	12%
Warner	11.9%	Universal	25.9%
Independents	25%	Sony	14.1%

Source: *The Recording Industry in Numbers*, 2003
IFPI annual yearbook

You will find a wonderful illustration of Warner Music's company structure on their website (www.warnermusiccareers.com). Take a look.

In the central circle of the illustration they list the following departments: International, Artist Relations, Human Resources, Finance, Business Affairs, Facilities, Sales/Production, New Media and IT. There are four boxes leading off from this circle: WEA London, WSM, EastWest Records and Warner Classics. Within those boxes are departments such as A&R and Marketing. It is a really instructive illustration.

All You Need to Know About the Music Business, by Donald S. Passman (published by Penguin) includes a chapter called 'Broad-Strokes Overview of the Record Business' which gives a helpful description of each department and a simple illustration of a record company. The author looks at a range of different companies from major to independent.

The *Music Education Directory* from the British Phonographic Industry (BPI) (www.bpi.co.uk) is an invaluable book which includes illustrated maps and flow charts of the four principal areas of the industry:

● the UK record company

● the UK music publishing company

● artist management

● UK live performance.

Each area is accompanied by descriptions of the jobs in each sector, which is very useful for you when exploring whether the music industry is for you..

CASH AND BLING AND SALES AND TING

According to the BPI, yearly album sales top £200m and have done since the mid 1990s.
Source: BPI, www.bpi.co.uk

Before looking at the needs of a band and the making of a CD and all the jobs in between, let's remind ourselves of the nature of the beast. How is the industry making money? Who is it targeting?

According to the BPI yearly album sales top £200m and have done since the mid-1990s but profits are down because of deals and price cutting in the high street. It looks like the industry is pulling one way and retailing is pulling the other.

Post-teen people, who are thought to have disposable income (money left after all the bills are paid), dominate the world of album-buying. Teens are thought to not have money-to-spend and this is sometimes cited as the reason for the collapse in the single-buying world.

Does that strike you as true? It might just be that the whole idea of the single belongs to yesteryear. Piracy, illegal copying and the demise of the single aren't new phenomena. What about copying from radio onto a cassette and the Walkman revolution? We were saying our goodbyes to the single even then. If you can make your own compilation why would you want a disc with one track on it – even with endless variations – for half the price of an album with its different tracks and bonus numbers?

> **The CD single market was worth £75.1m in the year from June 2002 to June 2003**
>
> **Source: BPI**

Perhaps the single will eventually disappear. Then again, didn't people say that of vinyl?

Nevertheless, look at the financial importance of the single market. According to the BPI it was worth £75.1m in the year from June 2002 to June 2003. The singles chart is the catwalk of the music industry and the album chart is where the serious shopping takes place.

'The year's total of 41m singles sales compares favourably with virtually every other country, but the fact remains that demand has halved within the last five years.'

Source: BPI spokesman in the *Guardian*, 18 August 2003

There are hundreds of articles on this subject on the Internet. Familiarise yourself with the arguments. For example, it is argued that those who download illegally from the Internet are actually no threat at all to the music business and its profits because those very people then go out to the shops to buy the album.

What do you think? What's your experience? What are your friends doing, buying or downloading? What branches of the industry are encouraging it? In chapter 6, 'Brave New World', you'll see how these arguments swirl around and give everyone a headache.

(Be careful about where you get your statistics from. The BPI has been dedicated to collecting industry data since 1973 so it's a good source. Newspapers and magazines may be arguing a line and following an agenda so be careful about what you base your opinions on. Take a look at the article 'Is Downloading Really Bad?', by Yinka Adegoke in the *Guardian* on April 5, 2004.)

Anyway, through all of the ups and downs it would seem that people still love to acquire music. It is still the case that a lot of our personality is expressed through our music preference and that it is important to us to have a collection that reflects who we are.

Do you have an enviable collection of vinyl and CDs? Do you devour the music magazines and follow bands or individuals through their concerts and trials and tribulations? If so, you'll know at first hand how successful the industry is in contributing to the flavour of our lives. It is really incredibly powerful.

SALES: HOW MANY MAKES MILLIONS?

How many CDs can a new artist expect to sell? Is the sky the limit? How many will a record company manufacture? According to Donald Passman's book, *All You Need To Know About The Music Business*, a new artist is someone who hasn't sold over 250,000 albums.

The International Federation of Phonographic Industries (IFPI, www.ifpi.org) gives figures for achieving Silver, Gold and Platinum sales for albums and singles.

Album and single sales

Albums: Silver = 60,000
                Gold = 100,000
                Platinum = 300,000
                Double Platinum = 600,000

Singles: Silver = 200,000
                Gold = 400,000
                Platinum = 600,000
                Double Platinum = 1.2 million

Source: IFPI

Passman's book is to be updated in 2005. Also, just to warn you, it is written from an American perspective but has sections on how the British music industry differs. It's a book that can apparently be found on many desks in a record company.

Ahmad Dayes, producer and studio engineer said that Passman's book taught him which terms to use and what equations and calculations the record companies make. Ahmad's training and career profile can be found in Chapter 5.

CHAPTER 3

Setting the scene

MAKING BANDS, SINGLES AND ALBUMS, AND MONEY

My first profile is about the band Moshikop. It shows the concerns of a new band and can be read with the eyes of a potential agent, manager, marketing assistant or lawyer. For other eyes, it gives a taste of what driving motivation and boundless energy people apply to their music making.

The second profile is of the band Clear and can be read with the eyes of a potential studio assistant, someone who wants to go into CD manufacturing, publishing and distribution.

CASE STUDY 1

I came across Moshikop recently at their first ever concert. The audience were rapt. I knew that the band was newly formed so I wanted to hear about their raw experiences for this book.

NB Think about this as we go through the interview:

● What can we learn from his experience of making music and pulling together his own band?

- If you were a potential talent scout or producer or band manager, what would you want to know from Moshik?

- How did he 'design' his band?

- What's his music and audience? Is it an audience you know? Does he have an agent or manager?

- Who is most relevant to his band's needs at the moment?

- If you were interviewing him, what would you ask?

'The most important thing I learn is: I always have more to learn.'

Moshik

Moshikop (www.moshikop.com) took their name from the lead member, Moshik, who is also the writer/producer. On stage he plays drums and percussion. He has already brought out a CD in Germany and, as a way of making money, is a sound engineer for another band, Oi Va Voi.

I wanted to know how the band came together. Was it formed by a collection of friends or were the individuals picked for a specific instrument or talent? How did they intend to promote their music? Will they take to the road for months on end? Will they cut a CD? I wanted to get their take on the music industry and the people in it. Who will be of use to them – lawyers, producers, managers? Are they waiting to be discovered by an A&R from a major label or do they have different ideas?

I asked Moshik about his musical background – what training did he have?

'I always had a strong passion for music. As a child I felt school was a waste of time. I quit high school at the age of 15 without having a specific direction, just the idea of making music. I started working in a PA company as a roadie, bought my first drum kit and I joined bands and singers to play, produce, compose, record and mix their albums and live shows. I don't have any formal qualification; I picked up drumming, producing, programming and sound engineering during the years so you can say I'm self-taught.'

Don't be eager to put the book down and march into school to announce your departure. Read to the end of the interview so you can appreciate exactly how much Moshik taught himself. Figure out for yourself if you are this dedicated and motivated and if you have the money to invest in the kind of equipment he talks about or if you are the type of person who needs the help and encouragement of a course.

I asked Moshik about his routine. Does he find himself doing 10 jobs at once, for his band and as a sound engineer for other bands?

'Being your own boss is the biggest freedom and at the same time it doesn't allow you to fit yourself into any routine. Working in the music industry is one of the most unstable jobs a man can get. I can find myself touring with one band, rehearsing and performing with another, producing a remix and composing a score for a play in one month, having no time to spend with my girlfriend at all, and a month later having more free time than actual work.

I love doing many different things. It keeps me alert and updated to what's going on in different scenes.'

One of his many jobs is as a sound engineer for Oi Va Voi. He's just finished touring with them so I asked what he learns from going on tour with another band that he can apply to Moshikop.

'Oi Va Voi are great musicians and above all amazing people. The most important thing I learn is: I always have more to learn. Keeping my mind open to new ideas, new or old music. That's what I love about this place; it's all part of the big game, getting to know new people and how to get along with them, wherever they're coming from.'

I asked Moshik how he pulled Moshikop together and whether he was looking for specific talents or just getting together with friends.

'I was doing my first gigs by myself, which I found boring and uninspiring so I started looking for a way to make it more live even though my music is very computer based. Some of the band's members are professional musicians who play with others, some are good friends. The band I want to create should be based on unconditional granting with no ego involved, therefore I would rather be surrounded by people I love than session musicians.'

Recap: If you are planning on working with a new band: what do you need to know? If you work for a record company, will this band appeal to the kind of audience your record company caters for? Perhaps the leader of the band will remind you of another lead person signed with your record company who has proven that there is a large following is there to be tapped?

I asked Moshik how he defines his music and what is his target audience? What are his influences? Does he follow trends?

'I don't have a target and don't like to think "yea, I should put down a Hip Hop track now". I started writing my music as a therapy. This is my only place to express unreachable feelings. I don't really try to define my music as it's just too eclectic. I love to call it Electro-Blues even though it's not a formal definition. I believe it's more of a crossover of down-tempo electronic and acoustic beats with some Mediterranean flavours. Cannot put my finger on any particular influence. I listen to loads of genres. It's not about what music I listen to, it's about what it makes me feel.'

Moshik already has experience of bringing out a CD with a record label in Germany. It was with Forte Records, a Techno/Electro label, and didn't suit Moshik's tastes.

I wondered if a new CD was planned, how he would do it differently and whether he's waiting for a label signing. Is there a time frame?

'Today I'm looking for a label that's dedicated to something more similar to what I do, something I can feel more attached to, than Forte Records. My second album is still in progress. All it needs is some good vocal tracks and maybe some songs. Most of it is instrumental. I've got my own home studio, which allows me to work whenever I want. I can wake up in the middle of the night with an idea and put it down straight away. I record only when I feel inspired but at the same time I need to have discipline. So far I've been working on this album for two years on and off. Finding a label will push me to shape my final touch to it I'm sure.'

Who else is on the scene? A manager? An agent? From the point of view of a band leader, I imagine they have very intense feelings about their music and therefore very critical opinions about the people they employ to help them.

'I don't have a manager but I know I need one. My music is not mainstream or radio-friendly so it'll be much harder for me to find one who knows how to deal with my stuff. There is an agent who helps me to find gigs, but again, I'm not falling into a category like "world music" or "electronic" which makes it difficult to place it in these sorts of festivals or events.'

The final question is one that I've put to all the contributors to this book in one way or another. I found Moshik's answer very refreshing and perhaps one to bear in mind when you read the daily reports of trouble caused by the new technology on the block.

The music press are all in a tizz about the changing nature of the biz. Are you? What difference has new technology and the Internet made to your experience of the music industry?

'New technology gave me as an individual the opportunity to create most of my music by myself, using virtual instruments alongside acoustic instruments, allowing me to manipulate sounds and having unlimited tools I could never afford. On the other hand you see more people ripping off music from the Internet. It's damaging us, the musicians, directly but I see no point fighting it. It's a beginning of an individualistic and free music-making trade market. It's still early days, it'll take more than a decade for us to see where it goes.'

Before moving on to another band that has been playing together for a while and cut their first CD, it's worth thinking about Moshik's concerns and the things he thinks he needs to push the band forward.

He thinks that a signing to a label will help his creative process. He thinks it will be hard to find a manager who will sympathise with his music. He thinks his music will give trouble to an agent who won't be able to place him in venues and festivals easily. Could you?

CASE STUDY 2

Here's a profile of a band that cut and financed their own CD. I thought it would be worth tracing their decisions and efforts. Why didn't they go the mainstream way? What did they give in to? What is the mainstream record industry doing when it puts off bands like this? Does creativity come out of hardship and rejecting the status quo?

The band is Clear and the lead singer and central character is Neil Ward-Dutton. Their website (www.clearweb.org) sums them up like this:

'Mark wanted nothing more than to write songs, Neil quite fancied the idea too. They tried it together. Craig loved what he heard – enough to move cities and join them.

Fast forward a few years . . . Clear have become really good. The record industry has gone from bad to worse. Clear's fan club, insistent that the band should release a record, have funded the band's debut album. They record the album 'Coming Round' in-between their day jobs. Record companies ask if they can release it. Clear pick the only one they trust.

Recent History . . . Clear's debut single released and gains international radio play and praise. Many DJ friends are made. Clear do first TV interview. Second single is released and gains further plays internationally and in the UK. Clear play acoustic sessions for UK radio.

Next . . . Clear are now working on a clutch of songs for a new album . . . it's shaping up to be a belter. Watch this space.'

Source: www.clearweb.org

And so to the studio and CD questions. I fired my questions at
Neil Ward-Dutton. In this interview I was more interested in
the process of making a CD. This throws up an entirely
different view of the music industry. Whereas Moshik was
thinking about the uses of a manager, an agent and the
creative possibilities of being with a label, Neil's concerns
were in another direction: which studio, which lawyer,
what money?

**Did you decide to cut a CD when you had tested the material at
gigs or did you write especially for the CD?**
'The answer is "half and half". We'd played around half of the
songs for a year or so at gigs, and the other half we ended up
writing as we were recording the first half. Basically we realised
our songs were getting increasingly strong, so we decided to
spend the second half of the process recording some new
material. Overall, we rehearsed/arranged around 20 songs in
total, in two batches, and recorded the two batches separately.
This was mainly for time reasons, because we all hold down day
jobs as well as being in a band.'

**How many gigs? How many reviews? How much part did
audience feedback play?**
'We'd been together for six years or so before we did the
album, so we'd done an awful lot of gigs by the point we
started. I think we probably wrote, played (and then ditched)
well over 30 songs before we even got to the point of
considering songs for recording. A lot of our early songs
weren't really that good.

'We relied a fair bit on audience feedback for the first few tracks
we recorded: as with most bands which survive longer than a
couple of years, you end up with some pretty loyal fans. But
you've got to be careful, and make sure you don't take too much
notice of your most ardent fans. Why? Because they'll love what
you do, even if it's not very good. It's actually very important to
get the views of someone who's at least partly independent, but
who's got experience.'

Do you have a manager/agent to help with decisions?
'This is where most would turn to a manager or agent for help.

We didn't have one, but we did have the help of an experienced producer/musician, Andy Metcalfe (who is perhaps best known as a member of Squeeze in the Eighties).'

Did you get a label signing or did you go it alone?
'We managed to hook up with a label which helped us with distribution and marketing but the recording was all self-funded through investments made by fans. The venture was featured on BBC 2's *Working Lunch*.

'It happened by accident. A fan asked the band if they were planning to produce a CD and offered to "lend" them couple of hundred pounds. The band members happened to mention the conversation to someone else . . . who also offered to lend money. The whole thing snowballed. In the end about 40 people offered money. Clear then set up a company and made the "fans" investors. That's how the money was raised and the fans are now waiting on the profits . . .'

Cutting the CD is just the first problem, though
'We manufactured 1,000 copies initially. Most manufacturers will do runs of fewer than 1,000 (say 500), but when you're paying for 500 you might as well go for 1,000 – the unit price drops considerably as you get to 1,000 units.'

Distribution?
'We took the album to a few labels and one, Invisible Hands Music (ihm), was interested in helping to distribute. That's how we got distribution. Finding a distributor can be the hardest thing to do.

'This is a very specialised area to get into and it's difficult to get a distributor to be interested in you. Distributors like predictability. Invisible Hands Music already had a relationship with a distributor so the matter was made relatively easy for us.

'Think about the job they have to do: distributors are gambling that they can get the right number of records to the right outlets at the right time. They work out the probable stock required by the various retailers, which retailers have an interested market, all in conjunction with the CD's airplay and marketing. They also operate on a sale or return basis. The distributor makes sure the retailer gets exactly what they need at the right time. If they get this wrong, they get the CDs back to clog up their warehouses.'

There are lots of names on the back of the CD: Abstraction Records, ihm, Universal. Who's who?

- Abstraction Records is the production company owned by Clear and a number of its fans (see above)

- Invisible Hands Music (ihm) helps Clear with distribution and marketing (www.invisiblehands.co.uk)

- ihm's distributor is Windsong, which is part of Universal.

Do you use the services of people you already know or people recommended?
'Both. This is probably the hardest part of trying to do anything serious in music. Many people in the industry are lazy, unprofessional blaggers. How do you know who is and who isn't?'

When does a band sort out the legalities?
'We've never hired a lawyer ourselves. ihm has the services of a commercial consultant (the ex-Managing Director of Factory Records) who helped us put together a very simple contract.'

You're not the first to be less than keen on taking the legal route. Why is this? Is it awkward to draw up a contract between friends?
'We considered it, in case of questions about royalties. We ended up drawing up a contract between ourselves in which we agreed to split everything equally, regardless of who wrote and who sang and who played.

'It's important that everyone is clear about what the position is. For example, what if one of the band members begins to write for someone else. Registering with MCPS (Mechanical Copyright Protection Society) or PRS (Performing Rights Society) means that you've taken a step into the administrative details but it's only when things go wrong that you need a lawyer.

'If you're going to go for a signing with a record company then you'll need to engage a lawyer to go through your contracts. You don't need to engage a lawyer on a retainer. (A retainer means that you pay them a fee regularly even when not using their services.)

'It's all got to come in the right order. There's no point getting stressed out about getting a lawyer or manager or agent. What you have to do before you get into any of that stuff is create a personality that people want to engage with. It has to be memorable; the songs, how you play, how you look and how you behave. That all has to come together and be convincing. Once you've got that right people will start taking notice and that's when you need to think about a lawyer.'

How long do you spend in the studio and what happens to the budget while you're there?
'We spent a total of around 30 days recording and mixing the album, in various studios. To keep the overall time down, we rehearsed like hell before we got into any kind of studio.

'Money just disappears when you're recording. It's very easy to spend lots and lots of it. We were playing with other people's money and it was important to spend it as carefully as possible. The overspend went on our underestimation of how long it would take to get things right in the studio.

'This is really important: before you set foot in the studio you must be able to play all your music backwards forwards and sideways without mistakes. You have to know what you want from a song. Obviously mistakes will happen but be careful. It's the songs that haven't been gigged that cause trouble.'

Here's what Clear learnt for the next time they find themselves recording in a studio – and paying top dollar by the hour:

● Spend the money where it's best spent – on drums and vocals

● Only hire a 'good' studio for drums (found by word of mouth). (Drums make the difference between a good record and a bad record.) Spend the money and get the perfection here then everything else is layered easily on top. Most other things you can record in your bedroom

- You will need extra budget for editing

- It's really important to find an experienced producer that you can trust. They'll protect you from a lot of rubbish and you'll learn a lot from them

- Save money by practising before the studio is booked.

AND SO TO THE RECORDING STUDIO

BEING A SOUND ENGINEER

For an insight to the life of a sound engineer I asked Neil Gardener, teacher at the Gateway School of Recording and Music Technology, to tell me everything there is to know. What are the hours? What are the thrills? What are the downsides?

For the rest of us, this is what we apparently should know about 'soundies'. They are, or course, driven by their passion, stuffed with talent and work ridiculous hours. They are full of stories but very honest, trustworthy and circumspect in professional circles.

What does Neil say about the whiz at the controls?
'It's a great job title, isn't it? An engineer of sound. You can hear the music, feel the excitement and almost see your name adorning the inlay sleeve of a top 20 CD. But what exactly does a sound engineer do? Well, it's a complicated answer, because sound engineers do a lot, and many of them do a lot in a lot of different areas of the music industry.'

SO LET'S TAKE A LOOK AT WHAT A SOUND ENGINEER DOES
Every album, single, piece of music on TV, radio or the Internet – in fact, everything you hear that is not live, has been recorded by a sound engineer. This is no easy job.

- You need to have a great pair of ears (and you must protect them – so no more standing next to the speakers in clubs, or listening to your iPod at full volume!)

● You need to love and understand music

● You need to have an interest in the technical side of music

● You need to be a great people manager.

In among all these things, you need to be able to record the live output of a band or musician and then reproduce it off tape, CD or computer in a way that doesn't misrepresent the artist's work. In essence, it is the sound engineer who takes the music from the musician and passes it along to the listener.

How does a sound engineer do all these things? Like most professions it comes with a lot of training and even more practice. The sound engineer must be able to control a recording studio confidently – everything from microphone selection and placement, through the understanding of acoustics and reverberation, past the control of a multi-channel mixing console, to the use of EQ, reverb, echo, distortion, and a host of other exciting sound manipulation tools.

Jargon box
EQ – equalisation for correction and sound enhancement in the wake of distortion
Reverb – when a signal is reflected as it would if in a cave. Unlike a delay, the quality of each sound is different
                Mixing & Recording Glossary (www.prosound.com)

The sound engineer also needs to understand the process of mixing different sounds together. Here is where you can specialise, as there are many sound engineers who only do recording, and those that only do the final mixing. The final mix of an album or track can make or break it – so this is generally another step up in the art of the professional sound engineer: your career progress to sound mixer.

The sound engineer needs to be able to set up and run the recording technology, be it for 2" master tape, recordable CD, or via hard disk systems and external hard drives. Sound daunting? If it does, maybe you should explore another area of production.

If you're getting excited, slavering at the mouth and shouting at the book 'I want to have go!', then you are perfect sound-engineer material. Why? Because sound engineering is a passion, a vocation. A four-minute song can take days or even weeks to record. You can easily spend a whole day just setting the microphones for a drum kit! And there's no slacking. If the artist wants to record through the night, then that's what you do.

For the engineer it's not so much sex, drugs and rock n roll, but decks, mugs of tea and sausage rolls!

In all this, the sound engineer is in the middle of things, ensuring everything works, sounds good and is being recorded. Without the sound engineer nothing would happen.

So if it's a dream job for those of you who love to twiddle knobs and play with studio equipment, what are the downsides? I mentioned people management earlier. The sound engineer needs to be a diplomat.

There's nothing more complex than the relationships between musicians, their friends, colleagues and music business types.

A recording session quickly becomes a tangled web of egos and arguments. You, as the sound engineer, must surf your way through this whirlwind of emotions, and deliver the quality end result expected. You must know what to say, when to say it and more importantly, when to keep out of things!

Then there's the constant repetition, of lyrics, drum loops, guitar breaks, etc. You think you like music? Some might say there's nothing worse than hearing the same 20 seconds of a song a hundred times over, day in, day out for a week – waiting while the singer or bassists work out how to get it just right. On the other hand, that's where the passion for the job kicks in.

And then there are the hours. Creating music is a difficult and time-consuming process that can go on for months. And when someone gets 'in the groove' the sound engineer can't turn around and say, 'But it's 6pm, I've gotta go home now.'

Bearing all this in mind, is sound engineering a good career? I have to say yes, it is, because I love recording, mixing and mastering. There's such a thrill to knowing that you're the person who made the music accessible to millions of listeners. Indeed, there's the thrill of being at the recording, with the musicians and experiencing the creation of new music. But there's also the joy of knowing that it was your decisions, technical and otherwise, that contributed to the final sound.

'Sound engineers make mammoth contributions to the overall feel of a track. They may not get the big name recognition of producers, but without them the recorded music wouldn't exist.'

The best musicians recognise the value of a good sound engineer and usually work with the same people year on year. This applies as much for live sound engineers, final mix engineers and the specialist-genre engineers (classical and jazz). It may not pay the most money, but you'll never go hungry.

If you want to become a sound engineer you should:

● Read sound engineering magazines such as *Sound On Sound* and *Pro Sound*

● Read as many sound engineering books as you can find

● Get involved with the live sound at a local club or live venue

● Listen to a lot of different styles of music and analyse them, work out how they were made

● Invest some time and money in getting qualified. Courses such as the Gateway School of Recording and Music Technology at Kingston University offer professionally recognised qualifications ranging all the way up to BA Honours.

Courses such as Gateway allow you to spend time in real studios, recording real bands under the guidance of professional and active sound engineers. You also learn about music business law, surround-sound mixing, live sound, hard disk editing, and sound for vision and MmI (Mobile mark-up language) technologies.

More and more, professional studios are seeking out young engineers with these qualifications, rather than taking on people who may be enthusiastic but lack hands-on experience.

THE RECORDING STUDIO

'We can't give work experience to anyone who doesn't have the technical basics. Why would we give a job as a runner to someone to just make tea for the artists? There's no point. They must want to progress and have the means of doing that.'

Andrea Terrano, Iguana Studios

Big studios are sponsored by major labels (like the Hollywood studio system of yesteryear) – the artists are in place and have proven themselves as big sellers, the facilities are in place, the mechanics of making the finished product are in place, the legal and financial systems are by and large dictated by the big companies and the finished product is assured to a certain standard for a certain market. It all works like clockwork. It's the traditional, conservative, status quo end of the studio spectrum. Abbey Road studios, for example, is one of the studios owned by EMI. Record company artists are fed through their own collection of studios.

According to Andrea Terrano, if you want to be a 'pure' engineer, this role really only exists in the record companies studios. To get work in a studio you could offer yourself as a runner from where you can hope to work your way up to tea maker, to tape operator, to assistant . . . and this is where you start getting a credit and really being involved.

Instead of writing a profile of the big, intimidating, packed-with-history studios I met Andrea Terrano who is the proud owner of the beautiful Iguana Studios.

I was interested in his perspective because of his experience of being in a band, studying sound engineering and becoming a teacher, and selling his flat to build a dream studio. With no financial backing, the studio was built almost brick by brick and with the help of friends and contacts that he made through his time in the music industry.

Andrea made it clear that I must tell you how important it is to be diplomatic and make good contacts. He said his studio couldn't have been built without help from friends and contacts made in the music industry.

The first thing you must know, according to Andrea, is that everyone in the industry who is an engineer is also a programmer. The competition is tough and you must be able to program on the major software platforms as a basic skill to offer the employer:

- Logic Audio (recommended)

- Cubase VST

- Sona

- Pro Tools.

Here is a description of one of the above. If you don't know the others, look them up.

Cubase is a complete virtual studio right there on your computer. You have a tape recorder, a mixer, effects processors, electronic instruments all in one integrated space. Of course, there is much more to Cubase than simply replacing outboard hardware. With Cubase, you have a powerful audio editing and sequencing environment at your fingertips.

www.cubase.com

Andrea can't give work experience to anyone who doesn't have the basics. Why, he asked me, would he give a job as a runner to someone to just make tea for the artists? There's no point. They must want to progress and have the means of doing that.

'If you are able to say that you are familiar with Logic it shows that you are ready for a job with a studio. The demand is huge for someone who knows what they are doing.

'You must be able to offer a good CV. Don't make it too colourful but don't make it dull.'

And here's something else, 'Be in the right place at the right time!'

I asked Andrea for his history in the music industry. He's been on a wonderful journey up to this point. He is a musician who is also a sound engineer. He says that when you add these two together you get a producer.

Andrea came from Italy as a musician to study English and sound engineering at the School of Audio Engineering (SAE). This venture was supported by his parents. He doesn't know if it would have been possible without them. This is important to him and he says that it is a great motivating force. When you finally make the break, it proves to your parents that they were right to put their faith in you.

At the same time he studied composition, took Grade 5 music theory and took harmony classes. In that sense, living in a city is ideal because of the access you have to short courses. Never underestimate the power of the teacher to be an industry contact. The composition teacher at Goldsmiths helped Andrea get a teaching job at Music Works (now Raw Materials) in Brixton.

The first break, however, and his first experience of employing the 'right-place-at-the-right-time rule', was when a friend saw an advert in *Loot* for a novice engineer for a home studio.

This was a magic break. This kind of ad, Andrea says, 'never comes up'. It proves that if you believe that you will make it, you will.

TOP TIP

You may have decided against formal training and formal qualifications. Moshik (in chapter 3) did exactly this. But remember that a teacher may be your first experience at making contacts and networking and may even be your access to the first magic break. A teacher will be your stimulus and will see your passion.

As a teacher at Music Works, Andrea took the chance to make a useful contact. He arranged to take his class out of the college environment and into a studio. He did some research, found a studio and introduced himself. The studio was Lion Music. He chose this one because they were still using the analogue system. It was the old-school way of working, with tape and not computers.

The introduction was successfully made, he got the job and worked in this old-world environment. He savoured the last of the pre-digital studio world and sponged up all he could learn about analogue and tape, quite apart from being surrounded by history and people talking about having worked with Bob Marley. It was the last echoes of an era.

You can see how Andrea would be so inspired to have his own studio.

All the while, Andrea was making additions to his home studio. Eventually he had a complete studio set up in his living room where his clientele and confidence grew. This is the beginning of the process that saw him eventually sell his flat and build his studio. He found a shell of a building and had enough vision and enough money for the task – and a sympathetic girlfriend willing to give him a home!

Iguana Studios staff
Andrea Terrano   Owner and manager
Tom Lindon   Chief Engineer and producer
Nigel Glasgow   Engineer

> **Iguana Studios clients**
> People cutting demos
> Mastering services for professionals
> Prolific artists who have a regular once-a-week booking
> An inexhaustible Hip Hop African artist called Ope
> The biggest name so far – Ministry of Sound who used
>   Andrea's own material

WHAT HAPPENS NEXT? HOW DO YOU MAKE A STUDIO WORK?

Andrea's strategy was to advertise in *Loot* for a few months. This costs, at present, £500 for approximately three months. It works as far as getting in the first few clients but now, he says, he needs to think of the next strategy in order to expand. That strategy needs to get the big companies interested.

AS THE MANAGER, ANDREA ALSO HAS TO KEEP GOOD ACCOUNTING BOOKS

He says that accepting cash-in-hand for jobs really doesn't help in the long run. When you finally go to the bank to ask for a business loan, you need to have a good track record of accounts which will prove that you are capable of bringing in work and turning around a professional business concern. Without a track record, how will a bank know what to make of you?

LAST WORDS OF ADVICE

- Don't give up

- Repay the work that the teachers have put in and the faith of your parents

- If you know how to use Logic, send Andrea your CV!

Where do you fit in?

WORK EXPERIENCE
'I think I got on really well with the people, I was willing to try really hard at even the most boring job they could offer and still have a laugh with everyone. I would go to any gig that had spare tickets which meant I got to talk to people outside the office environment, quite often I could chat and have a few beers with the MD of Sony International, time and advice I never would have got during office hours.'
    Sam Elderidge (see 'Profile of a Band Manager', page 40)

WHERE TO FIND WORK EXPERIENCE

Your school might send you to a record company and you'll have to cope for a week or two in the office environment where people are likely to be too busy to take your fledgling career by the hand and lead you into the big time.

You could call up and ask for some kind of job description to prepare yourself but companies might just be too busy and, really, they will want you to run around, send out mail and generally make yourself useful.

This might not light your fire but don't forget that you are in the privileged position of being on the inside, seeing how a company works; in conversations that fly back and forth you'll hear what kind of knowledge people have about the industry, you'll hear their telephone conversations and their negotiations. Make notes. Ask questions.

To prepare for the work experience make sure you've read the industry magazines to inform yourself. This is an industry full of very confident people with very strong opinions and who are tireless in their 'work hard/play hard' duties. Don't be daunted. Dive in. Have a go.

I made a call and got some work experience advice for you. I called Alice Schofield at Anglo Plugging. Here's some information about Anglo Plugging from their website:

THE ANGLO METHOD
At Anglo we provide national and regional, radio and TV promotion as well as online promotion. In consultation with artist management, press agent and record company we will assess the areas of exposure that can be realistically achieved whether an artist is looking for their first radio play or is about to embark on a fifth album launch.

With a promotion company you are primarily buying time, contacts and expertise. As chart success increases so too does the workload and time involved dealing with an artist. The media is constantly changing with new radio stations, new TV shows, new websites, etc. it is vital for us to stay on top of all these developments, this means we can be best informed when it comes to selecting release dates or the timing of events.

We use computer tracking to list all radio station plays, as it is crucial to have up to the minute information in the early stages of breaking of a record, particularly on regional radio. We also have our own website which contains artist info plus links to other music sites.

Source: www.angloplugging.co.uk

Alice is the contact for work experience people at Anglo Plugging. I asked her for her thoughts on the subject. First of all I asked her to describe a work experience person who had really impressed everyone. Here's what she said:
'We had a girl called Sasha in for work experience one week about a year back. She was 16, doing her GCSEs, not necessarily planning on being in the music industry but was keen to learn all the same. She was friendly, chatty and above all helpful. You could always rely on her to do any job for you no matter how menial it was. She really fitted in as part of the team and it was just a shame we had to let her go at the end of the week.'

So, how exactly did she shine? What if you find, horror of horrors, that you have nothing to do? Should you go around asking who else you can help? How can you impress? Alice says:
'The best advice I can give is to be proactive. Never sit there with nothing to do, always ask around if there's anything you can do to help. Always be prepared to do menial tasks and carry them out to your best ability, never show you are bored or unhappy with any task you've been given, always come across as happy to help.

'Asking questions is the best way to learn, but the pupil must also realise that we have a job to do, so they can't be asking questions all day! I've always been impressed with pupils that are keen to know exactly what we do, and how to go about getting into this job.'

I asked Alice what jobs are always there to be done. There are three main things:
'Stickering up and mailing out CDs and records. A work experience person will mainly be helping with mailouts as this is the bulk of our job. Other jobs they may be given are things such as typing up press releases and tour dates and, of course, filing.'

Yes, but who is the work experience likely to be with? Marketing? Plugging? Do they go offsite to radio stations?
'They will work with the plugging team. No chances to go out to stations unfortunately, but if we are doing an event they may be asked to come and help out there.'

PITFALLS

You need to know more than anything what *not* to do, what behaviour and attitude will not impress. I asked Alice about a disappointing time with a student.

'There was a guy who asked if he could come in for work experience. Before he started he was told that we wouldn't pay any expenses and that the main work would be mailing out records. When he came he kicked up a fuss and was rude, left after two days and then wrote an email to our head of promotions complaining. We replied that had he stuck it out he would have found that he would have been given more things to do, plus he should realise that in every job you need to start at the bottom, nothing should be below you.

'He left us with a very sour taste in our mouths and I am very careful now about people who I take on. I make sure they know that they will be doing a lot of menial tasks. This does not mean these tasks are not an important part of learning about the job. The best way to learn is starting at the bottom and working your way up and taking it upon yourself to learn about the job by asking questions and seeing how others work.'

'Another example of someone who didn't impress was a girl that came in and didn't say a word for the whole week, never came up and asked for things to do, would just sit there reading a magazine until you asked her to do a job, when she'd finish she wouldn't say "I've finished" . . . she would just go back to reading the magazine.'

'A work experience person should be more proactive. I like a work experience person to enjoy their time here, but it really is a lot to do with them and how they approach the job. A happy, smiley and chatty person is likely to get along much better than someone who's quiet and unconfident.

'A work experience person should make the most out of their week by asking questions and being proactive, always be prepared for doing boring jobs!'

Alice is really emphasising the 'menial', 'boring', 'start-at-the-bottom' warning. My impression of this is that they've seen work experience people who were disappointed with their time and Alice wants to make it clear that you won't be running the company in your first week. Nevertheless, you have to impress. You're finding out about the world of work and there are things you must do in all walks of life from nine to five.

- Always be on time. Lateness is not impressive.

- Always employ manners: knock on doors before entering, say 'excuse me' if you urgently have to interrupt a conversation, or 'sorry to bother you but . . .' if you're asking for help or another task.

- You could offer to get a round of coffees for your colleagues.

- Greet people properly in the morning and make sure when you leave that you haven't left work undone or an untidy desk behind.

- Always be polite to colleagues, from the receptionist in the morning to the late-night cleaners.

These are basic qualities that everyone at any age in any job should observe.

CHAPTER 5

Job profiles

PROFILE OF A BAND MANAGER

Sam Elderidge is the manager of Ludes, an R&B outfit who are celebrated on various websites and in music press articles as 'just what the music business needs right now'.

When reading up on managers of bands a few common themes emerge. I put these points to Sam. Many managers seem to know key members of a band from school and get roped in to doing all the jobs other than music-making. This is a happy accident if managing a band is your goal.

I asked Sam how he met Ludes and if there's a problem being professionally associated with friends.
'Managing Ludes was a kind of great accident, like a lot of things in music. I knew the guitarist James and just thought it would be good to have something of my own outside of my job at Sony. I started doing it part-time until it became a full-time job and it turned into a career when we got our deals and started earning a bit of money as well.

'You can get too close to an act and lose some vital critical distance, or if you are mates to start with you might fall out over

the sometimes harsh realities you have to offer the band. The
best thing is to keep some distance and separate the biz side
with the mates side and, as long as everyone is clear where that
line is, all should be cool.

'But don't expect it to happen overnight. Quite often the biggest
bands have been quietly slogging away for years before anyone
hears a note.'

What does a manager do to marshal a gaggle of friends into a serious performing outfit?
'It is a case of encouraging them creatively and putting them at
the right venues at the right time. There are loads of clubs in
London where all the A&R guys go, they tend to hunt in packs,
but a manager has to choose the right time to go there. You have
to be confident that you have created a following and that the
band's material is as strong as it could be.'

Where did you get this knowledge from: to know the venues, to know how to build up a fan base, to know what the right time is?
'During my time at Sony press office, I got a great insight into
why some bands capture the public's imagination and others just
don't. This led me to want to work in A&R where you actually find
those bands and work with them on the creative side. A&R really
opened my eyes to what a band needs to achieve in terms of plot
and strategy to become successful and get signed.'

Check out page 43 to find out more about A&R.

Donald Passman's book, and other band manuals, go into great
detail about getting a team together and I wondered how
accurate this is for the beginners. Sam confirmed that getting
Ludes to their present position was all about putting together the
right team.

I asked Sam who his team were and where they came from.
'As well as A&R people you will often find independent press and
promotion people as well as agents at the right gigs. These
people will sometimes offer to work for free at first so they can
be involved when the band "breaks".

'There are quite a lot of independent press and promotions people around and it is a question of research: seeing which artists they represent; would you like to be associated with those artists and; has the PR and marketing worked well for them?

'Once you have your team (press – getting you in the magazines; promo – pushing you to radio and television; agent – booking your gigs) the manager's job is to co-ordinate all these aspects so they are all driving towards the same point at the right time, generally around a single or album release.

'Aside from this you have a lawyer and accountant who can be instrumental in getting you the right deal and pushing you to the best people; again they will often hang out at key venues to pick up bands.'

What about getting signed?
'Generally the bigger companies have more power and so can push your band into the right areas. However, small companies may treat you as a priority and work even harder for you. I guess it's all a question of what fits the band.'

Building up a fan base? How?
'We have street teams of young kids in each town who hand out flyers, get emails off of fans, and generally raise awareness of the band in their town. This can be a great way for younger people interested in the music business getting some contact with people at record companies.

'To build up a local fan base try and do something original that sets you apart from the crowd. No real point touring till you have some sort of press, radio play and a fan base.'

Touring?
'Our tour was booked through an agent, who knows what size venues we can fill according to the band's profile. The tour was quite heavily supported by Xfm (a London radio station) and *NME* so guaranteeing some support.'

Pitfalls and rewards?
'It can take over your life. It's not a 9–5 job. I have recently taken

on a couple of new acts, a new office and I'm looking to set up a studio with my partner. It's all a case of building slowly but surely and in a business where there are no set rules. I was an intern one week and manager the next. It's a case of going for every opportunity however small it may seem.'

New technology? The music press are all in a tizz about the changing nature of the biz. Are you?
'The Internet has had a massive effect on the music business and my job is to react positively to this be it with downloadable singles, ringtones or whatever. Like everything else, as a manager you've got to see how best you can rig it to your band's advantage.'

EXPLORING THE ROLE: A&R (ARTIST & REPERTOIRE)

Do you think you can spot a hit, understand the trends, uncover bands that will take the scene by storm, enthuse new talent and smooth their way to stardom, and are confident that you can make the label, your employer, money? Then take a look at a career in A&R.

It's your turn. Conduct the next interview and write up the job profile. Find an A&R person and say you're doing an article for *XYZ* and you are looking for careers advice. Write the article and get it published in your school, college or local paper as a career exposé article. Give it a try.

Do some research on the role of A&R and then call up record companies and ask to be put through to their A&R department. Make your contact, explain that you're writing an article and ask if they have a couple of minutes for an interview. They might have time to meet and you might feel confident enough to ask your questions and take notes under their gaze. If not, offer to send the questions via email if it would be of more help to them (remember how busy they might be at that moment) then you can make a follow-up call if there's anything you need to add or clarify. Do the interview and get the article published. Perhaps you can then go back and try to organise work experience. See how you do.

The BBC's *Top of the Pops* website has a 'Music Biz' guide where you can find a guide to A&R by clicking on a picture of *Pop Idol's* Simon Cowell (www.bbc.co.uk/totp/music_biz_guide). This site may be updated and move on, in which case simply type into your search engine "A&R Career UK" and see what you can find. Look at the familiar sites like *TOTP* and BPI. These sites will have sound and genuine advice.

As part of your research, take a look at *AandRonline* magazine. (www.aandronline.com)

What are some things that artists can do to get themselves noticed? I found this quote on:
www.record-labels-companies-guide.com/
article-record-label-101.html

'Create a following and a story. Things that would contribute to a story would be various data that we could track – sold-out shows, record sales, and getting airplay on their own. That happens all the time. Those are things that virtually all A&R people look for.'

Tom Sarig, Vice President,
A&R MCA Records

EXPLORING THE ROLE: PROFILE OF A PRODUCER

'Once you get into the realm of putting your ideas down, you are producing.'

My next case study is Ahmad Dayes.

'As a producer Ahmad Dayes creates backing tracks for vocalists. He runs the recording sessions and also mixes the tracks. He's been producing since he was 18. Since summer 2002 he's been producing with, and for, vocalists, varying from hip hop, R'n'B, drum and bass to more party-orientated tracks. Some of the tracks that have come about can't really be put in a category, which is a good thing as he is always trying to create the next new sound. His music draws in a lot of classical influence; this has probably come about through playing in orchestras and symphonic bands from an early age. Playing the trombone and piano has also proven to be a great source of originality and inspiration to him. His long-term ambition is to break through to the main stream and set up his own record label.'

Source: Midi Music Company
(77 Watsons Street, Deptford, London, SE8 4AU)

'The reason that I got into producing and engineering was in order to make drum and bass music. It's not a genre of music that is really possible to create without using some sort of music technology.

'I had a brief encounter with Cubase when I was at school. So I had a very vague idea of how it might be possible to start making tunes. I was lucky enough to meet someone who made drum and bass. Through regular visits I started to pick up how the process worked in putting a tune together.

'The next stage for me was to start training myself in the skills needed to operate a studio. The first and still one of the most important things I had to learn was how to operate a computer with music software.

'I enrolled on an evening Cubase course which taught me the basics I needed to know to start putting my ideas down. Once you get into the realm of putting your ideas down, you are producing.

'I found that once I was making tunes, and taking them away to listen and work on them again, the learning curve got quite steep. Your ears start to develop a taste for sounds and rhythms quite fast.

'But one thing that I remember doing a lot more was listening to other people's music and working out how they put together their tunes.

'If I was really going to make tunes seriously I would need some equipment to get me started. Strategically the one piece of equipment that was really going to help me would be a computer. Ever since I had my own computer I have been able to make music when I want and how I want.'

When that special idea comes around and you get it down you know what it's all about.

'My next move was to enrol on a course at the Midi Music Company (MMC), which looked at the creative aspect of making music at the same time as the technical side. Being on that course really opened up my head as I started getting experience working with and for other people. I enrolled on other courses that went further into the studio side of the process. After I knew what I was doing in the studio I was asked to help out and do a bit of vocal recording for another course that was going on.

'I felt like I had been thrust into the deep end at the time but looking back that is the fastest way to learn. Being involved at MMC has given me a base to work from. I started to make music for vocalists of different styles and found that they brought something to my music that I couldn't get when making purely instrumental tracks.'

One of the ways that I work is to give vocalists a selection of ideas on a CD to pick over. When they have got comfortable with that idea and have written something for it, we lay it down on computer. This really enables me to get into the tune more. It creates the bigger picture.

'Being involved with MMC has given me a good base to work with people and really get into the music. One of the reasons I was able to get free studio time was that I did a lot of volunteering for them and looked after the equipment. Plus MMC is an organisation set up to help young people get involved in the music game.

'Through working with other people and trying out new ideas you pick up the skills needed to make it a profession faster. As an independent producer you have to be an engineer as well as producer. The two go hand in hand because if you can engineer you save a hell of a lot time and money creating a finished piece of music (the job of the producer).'

'As inspiration is somewhat of a random thing, it is very important to be able to get that idea down when it comes to you; if you don't have the skills to put that idea down when you get it you lose it.'

'It's strange that there are infinite possibilities with music yet you can go weeks without getting that spark. Even when you get that spark, it can seem impossible to finish the tune.

'Through putting yourself through the motions you pick up all the details that count. By making yourself available to work on a regular basis you learn much faster and get more comfortable with your working environment.

'You can't expect to learn the theory and then be able to go out and make a living from it. Experience, experience, experience is what gets you where you want to be, so you've got to grab and make opportunities for yourself to gain that experience.

'Everyone has their own way of doing things. It's about finding yours and constantly adjusting it to work in all situations.'

EXPLORING THE ROLE: MARKETING MANAGER

Oliver X is a product manager with a major record company.

The marketing department of a record company is *the* cool place to be. Oliver lives a life of wild European travel and after-show parties. He mixes with artists and gets loads of free CDs. He always has lovely clothes, great haircuts, discovers and frequents the best venues. I want to be him! I asked him how to do that. I discovered that it would take planning, focus, mountainous motivation, patience and money for countless phone calls.

First he studied marketing and business techniques – for his degree (BSc in European Business and Technology) before studying for a Master's degree in Sales and Marketing from the University of Montpellier in France. During his studies, he lived in France, Spain and the UK. His mother tongue is French but he moved around to improve his languages. He finished his studies by the time he was 22.

He worked in a medical equipment company after graduating but was a DJ at parties and weddings and spent his spare time reading all the music weeklies and magazines. He was always looking for contacts in the radio and music industry and at 23 sent CVs to Paris, London, Madrid, and Barcelona where he knew a music scene existed and was active.

He chased up every CV with phone calls – nobody returned his calls! All the companies sent rejection letters back. Finally he got through to a live body at a radio production company in London who suggested he come to London for a meeting, without making any promise of work!

He made the trip. He found a backpackers' hostel in London, visited the production company and made more calls to employment agencies that specialise in music.

At the radio production company he was offered two weeks' paid work to cover somebody's holiday leave at £200 a week and he took it. That was in the last two weeks of June 1997 – after which he was offered a job as Marketing Assistant.

After years of photocopying, packing, translating, coffee-making and waiting for couriers, my friend was ready to move on.

What did he learn from the production company?
'That the media is full of very ambitious people and if you want to learn you have to learn a lot by yourself and not rely on others. You need initiative.'

He learnt how to negotiate to sell programmes to radio stations around Europe. He applied sales and marketing techniques learnt during his studies. After a few years at the company he was promoted to International Sales Executive but his salary didn't match the swanky title, rising from £10,000 to £18,000 in four years by March 2001.

Why did he stay so long in a radio production company when the music industry was his first choice? He used it as a platform to reach record companies later. He chose a parallel field when the right opportunity wasn't available in the music industry.

This is a really interesting part of his story . . . the diligence that went into making his move into the music industry. Between the decision of leaving the production company and arriving at the door of the record company he took six months of planning and laying the groundwork. He spent the time going to tons of concerts and set up meetings with heads of radio plugging companies. He thought he would move into the plugging business but was advised that the salary wouldn't increase too much and that he might be overqualified.

He was advised to write to record companies directly and apply to their marketing departments. He wrote to the heads of the international marketing sections of the major record labels.

So, again, he went through the routine of writing letters, meeting lots of artist managers, arranging meetings and going to concerts

Why is it important to go to all kinds of concerts - ones he liked and ones he didn't?
'It's important to meet and network with people from different circles, ones you are not necessarily interested in or that are consistent with your taste in music. You must always be aware of increasing your contact list.'

Oliver spent the evenings at concerts observing the audiences; the profile of the audience. He tuned in his mindset to what is being played on different types of radio, on MTV, what's being played in clubs, what people are buying and what's in the charts compared to what is played in bars, clubs and in the street.'

After a few interviews he landed a job with one of the major record companies. He got a call from a director of marketing who was very interested in meeting him. He says his experience in the radio production company made him an attractive prospect to have in a marketing department.

This is the beginning of the next journey. The record company made him jump through hoops before offering him a job as a junior product manager. It took four interviews!

He had a meeting at the office of his future boss and then was invited for a second meeting with the boss's boss. He knew he had to really impress this one. He was asked questions such as which kinds of music he liked. How honest was he in answering this question? It's an obvious question but he wasn't prepared for it so he was vague and named a few acts.

He said he had varied tastes. He didn't want to be pigeon-holed. He was also asked to name the last five CDs he had bought. This showed that he was an active follower of music and spent his hard-earned cash on his interest.

I returned to the question of what kind of music he likes. I wanted the perfect answer from him.
'A good answer is not to be too specific. You must show varied tastes and an open mind. Show you are interested in going to concerts and name the most recent ones you've been to.'

In both of the initial interviews he had to go through his career and explain his choices.
'It's important to build your CV and not appear as if you've arrived by chance at this point. If people see you have an ambition and an objective they are more likely to give you the job.'

As if two meetings are not enough, he was called for a third meeting. This was to meet up with his original contact, just to confirm that the boss was very interested in employing him. Having got this far, the head of Human Resources had to be involved. This is where he was put through a series of knowledge and personality tests.

Be aware of the psychometric test. I have to say, Oliver is the only person I've ever heard of who had to take one. You have to answer as many questions as possible in the shortest possible time. There are sections in CV and interview books that will cover it.

So, Oliver is this funky, fashionable person who travels Europe . . . He objects – most of his work is email and office-based. Once or twice a month he has to travel to meetings or concerts abroad but there's no rule to that. He works hard and long hours every day but it's still a dream job.

Did he think he would reach his dream job quicker than this?
'Yes! How naive I was to think I could right away work for a record company fresh out of university. But I don't regret having worked in the radio industry and still use my knowledge of the international radio scene. Today when I review marketing plans from various countries for the artists I'm in charge of, it allows me to be more critical especially regarding the radio strategy.'

Ok, this looks to me like a lot of studying, a lot of hard work, a lot of time spent in a job that was not his first choice and a lot of research (travel, concerts, meetings) on his own budget.

Was it worth it?
'Well, it is important to be motivated and focused on the professional objective.'

Postscript
If you are wondering why I haven't named Oliver's company, it's because he just lost his job. The company 'restructured' and got rid of over a thousand people. My friend's skills,

commitment, enthusiasm, towering experience and the fact
that he was popular and respected among all his colleagues
mattered not a jot. But I do think it will help him breeze
into his next job.

EXPLORING THE ROLE: ARTIST/DJ MANAGEMENT

Plenty is written about artist management. In this book Sam
Elderidge has given his testimony on running a band and how to
do it. There are books being published right now with very
scintillating stories about working with all-time heroes by having
the nerve to simply ask the artist in question.

Paul Charles wrote *The Complete Guide to Playing Live* (Omnibus
Press) which is an autobiographically based 'how to' book.
Through his own experience he covers finding agents, managers,
lawyers and the book is promoted as 'the ultimate manual for
survival on the road'.

I like this book a lot and it's probably the kind of book you should
take a look at to broaden and deepen your general knowledge as
well as pick up a few tips but, I have to say, when hot-off-the-press
books like this give examples of managing bands, it's all a little
old-fashioned. Paul Charles talks about heroes such as Tom Waits.
To get a funkier picture of the music industry and how it works, DJ
books are at least up to date with examples they use.

While reading through this book you'll have taken the advice by
the horns and conducted an interview with the A&R person, you'll
have had it published in your school or college or local paper and
you'll have promised them a 'Careers Exposé' series.

So the second in your series could be artist management. There
are all kinds of questions you could ask about how a manager
has to run around to satisfy the tiniest and silliest needs of a
superstar-type. I think you'll find, also, how closely a good team
can work together and how mutual respect between band and
manager can flourish.

You could also try to find the manager of a DJ instead of a band manager. I've put together some questions but don't use these if you can spend time on working out the questions for a more creative and targeted interview.

QUESTIONS FOR A DJ AGENT

● What does the manager of a DJ do?

● Tell me about a DJ you're managing at the moment.

● What kinds of considerations are there in starting out with a new DJ? Or will you only take on established DJs?

● In the context of being at school or university, how can the would-be manager convince a DJ that they need a manager?

● Is the music scene at the moment conducive to starting as a manager?

● How did you start?

● Do I have to head for a course in management or does the music industry like self-taught people?

● What are the tools of the job? (Contacts book? Mobile phone with lots of free minutes? Sympathetic parents?)

● OK, what do I do now? Where do I start? What should I read?

PROFILE OF DJ NIKKI

I ran some questions by a DJ so that you can see the mindset of a DJ to help you in your research. DJ NIKKI from beatniktv.com, on Sky digital 184, is 'one of the major rap DJ playas on London's scene'. When you read articles about her it's amazing and inspiring to see the superlative quotes about her skills, her entrepreneurship and her creativity.

Articles about DJ NIKKI:
www.ministryofsound.com/Music/DJFeatures/
DJNikkibiography.htm
www.beatniktv.com/profiledjnikki.html
www.rwdmag.com/music_articles/features/
04940-794867/dj_nikki/

If you're wondering what the difference is between the club
DJ and the studio producer and what career progression
there is once you've hit the clubs, read these articles.

Here are a couple of things I learnt about her from those articles:
she went to music school when she was seven years old so she's
classically trained in piano and cello (she'll include some cello
playing in her sets!); she was a DJ throughout her time at
university (she studied Fine Art, painting and sculpture); she has
a 21-year-old brother who started DJing at 12 years old!

This may explain why her answers to my questions give no room
for consideration of anyone who is a total beginner. If you're
starting out as a DJ, especially in one of the country's smaller
towns or in a village, you will have to consider how to pick a
venue, what audience research you have to do, what you have to
know about the policy on the door, what about guest lists and all
kinds of practicalities.

DJ NIKKI is so long established that all those details are passé!
My questions were targeted at finding answers for the novice.
From her answers it looks like the DJ world is just so competitive
that you'll have to be a novice elsewhere and hit the scene in full
control of your craft.

Instead, her answers give her views on the jobs of promoters, A&R
managers and agents. Overall you will see what a business it is to
be a DJ and what business awareness you need to run yourself
and your decks as a company. You'll notice, though, that some of
her answers won't apply to the local venue in your town or village.

PRACTICALITIES

How do you pick a venue?

I work off recommendation and word of mouth or through my agency/business partner.

Do you visit the place for the first time on the night of performance or should it be a place you're familiar with?

I personally never visit a club first. I should be good enough at my job not to have to do this.

How well should you already know the crowd?

As a DJ, experience tells you what each crowd will be and so which records to pack. Also I know nearly every venue in London certainly and round the UK so I will vary my sets accordingly.

What else do you look for?

A sound system that works (although this rarely happens).

What are the possible pitfalls?

Promoters not paying a DJ. This, however, does not happen to me.

How much do you need to charge on the door? (Should it cover your costs or is it the normal entry fee – do you have any say?)

I do not get involved as a DJ in what a promoter charges. It is up to them to make money from actually promoting the night. DJs do not get a say in this usually. However, if it is my night and I am DJing then I would control every aspect of the night from door staff to charges to wages.

Who's collecting? What happens if costs aren't covered by takings – whose fault is it?

If costs aren't covered it's down to the promoter – nothing to do with the DJ.

Are you paid up front ever or is it all based on takings at the door or bar?

I am always paid upfront unless I know the promoter really well and have a relationship built up over years.

FRIENDS OR FOES
All your friends want to go on the guest list – how long should a guest list be?

My friends know better than to ask for guest list everywhere. I have worked as a DJ for over 10 years and run clubs in London for over 5 years. It is a business. I will never take liberties with promoters to get my friends on the guest list. If I am DJing and at artist after-show parties (e.g. P. Diddy, Mariah) I will take my business partners with me (maximum 2 people).

Is there a chance of being seen by A&R, or agents and managers?

A&R people and managers all come to places I DJ at anyway. I have many friends and business associates who do these jobs. We all help each other out if we can.

In terms of agents or managers, if you work with your friends, what can you do about the dead weights?

There is no room for dead weight if you want to run a successful company – same with DJing. It is very competitive. Only those who have a realistic grip of business will survive.

TRANSPORTATION
Exactly how much equipment are you transporting? How often do you take your own decks or do you presume every venue has decks you can use?

I have not taken decks to a venue or party since the late 80s! All clubs/bars these days will have decks. Many even have CD decks, too, of the highest quality. So it is never required that I take equipment.

How many records are enough for how many hours?

100 records per hour is how I tend to work. Even though I do not play that many, I will take one box for each hour so that if another DJ has the same record selection I can always bring out something extra.

How much time do you take to set up before the show?

It is professional to hear the previous DJ's set.

QUIDS IN OR QUIDS OUT?
Finally, how would having an agent help?
Does not help at all.

What would you want from an agent?
Do not use agents.

Do you presume that they are also DJs part of the time?
Most are.

Is there a book you can recommend?
No book can teach you this. Practise!

DJs are possibly the busiest people I've come across in finding contributors for this book – they always seem to be flying abroad for a gig! If I'd had the time it would have been worth asking DJ NIKKI for her take on the difference between male and female DJs.

To get another approach to DJing I spoke to DJ Simon at Momo's in London. His enthusiasm for his craft was infectious.

'To break into DJing you must break onto the scene with something new: a new act, a different mix, a unique selling point. Get to know your venues well. Make demos and send them to gigs. Don't sent your best hip hop mix to every club in town if you live in a seaside resort which only caters to twee disco tastes. Think about targeting venues and marketing yourself. Equipment is all-important. 'DJ In A Box' (the packaged turntables available on the high street) is not professional enough. Too many DJs can play in the bedroom but can't work a crowd and read an audience. Think about the DJs who have made it big. What background did they come from?'

DJ Simon, Momo's in London

EXPLORE THE ROLE – MUSIC PUBLISHING
Look at the website of the Music Publishers' Association. Below is a list of Frequently Asked Questions that you can visit to access very detailed answers.

What is music publishing? What is copyright? How do I protect my music? Who should I send my music to? How can I locate a piece of printed music? Can I photocopy printed music? Can I make arrangements of original music? Can I sample or quote from someone else's music? How can I find the copyright owner for permission to use a piece of music? What should I do if I believe that someone may be infringing copyright? How can I find out more about a career in music publishing? How do I form a music publishing company?

Source: www.mpaonline.org.uk/faqs/what_is_pub.html

EXPLORING THE ROLE – VENUE MUSIC DIRECTOR

Laure Malca is the Music Director (or programmer) for Momo's. It's a world music club for members only and has the best bands in the world lining up at its door. It's the only club in London dedicated to world music so you would expect the audience to be very particular and the music director to be quite a specialist. There are lessons you can take from her story and apply to any music venue.

Well, Laure didn't take an obvious route into a music career but it's one that she combined with her passion for music. She was a journalist and editor in Paris for *Nova*, which is the equivalent of *Time Out*. 'Journalism will always stand you in good stead,' she says.

As a teenager she was always following live bands and all her friends were musicians. She watched as they had to do everything themselves: they produced packages of their music and sent them to promoters; they organised their own live shows; they built their own country-wide tours, then European tours; they existed on paltry finances; they did everything an agent would be expected to do. Laure's education in the workings of a band came before her university education! She understood their point of view. She went on tour with them and existed in their van with them. She saw the funky side of life on the road.

'To be in the environment of a musician is important. You must love music. Also, specialisation in a genre is important. Otherwise, how will you acquire credibility or enough knowledge? Otherwise you will be lost.'

Well, she's right. You already know where your interest lies. You already know the difference between country music and Hip Hop. Her main advice is to build up a contact list in the same way a journalist collects contacts . . . greedily. She gives this example of how to get started:

'If you have never done this before or you're new to the area or city, find a music magazine or listings magazine and check the "on the road" section.' (Such as *Soundwaves* Magazine, a World Music essential.)

'There's a flamenco band at Sadlers Wells theatre and I'm interested in this band for Momo's. I would call the magazine for a contact; they would put me on to the venue. You must make the calls. As in journalism, you are on the phone a lot of the time.

'If there's a CD you like, call the distributor and ask for a contact for the band. Get the number for the band's agent. You need powers of persuasion!'

To get a band to perform at your venue you must know what you're talking about:

● Is the band well known – are they respected with their genre?

- How many CDs have they produced?

- Is there a new CD?

- Are they doing a promotion tour?

- Is your venue relevant to their audience?

- Will they get sales or publicity – what is the point for them to perform at your venue?

- Know your field!

- Always listen to CDs – it sounds obvious but needs to be said. This isn't part of the job that can be skipped!

Organisation on the day of the performance.

'This is a job for people who can keep on top of many tasks and many demands. When the band have agreed to perform at your venue you have to agree a date, a fee. You may have to organise hotel and catering, equipment may need to be rented, you might need to employ a sound engineer and organise a sound check. You have to be present at the sound check. If the band members have any complaints, you've been their contact and their grievances will come back to you.

'All of this may be perfect but means nothing without publicity. Get a biography of the group and a picture, write a press release, if you don't have a contacts list in the press to send your press release out to . . . make one. Target the journalists in the music press that you've been reading so avidly. Find out who to target in the local press and local radio.'

Here's what Laure recommends for aspiring music directors:

'Find voluntary work with a music director. That's one possibility. Otherwise, at university you can organise bands with the Student Union. Otherwise, be innovative and find a café in your town or village that will let you use it as a venue. You could find work as a volunteer or in some capacity in a venue or working for a touring agency. Have a go.

'Here's what you will find out: you'll learn all about making calls, you will learn about being a diplomat and holding the purse strings very tightly. You'll learn about how a band operates.

'As you proceed further into the experience of a music director you'll come across bands that are organised, professional and have developed into a functioning entity with a label, a publisher, a distribution company, a touring agent and a tour manager.

'You'll need to learn about all these roles, how it all works, where you fit in and who you need to negotiate with.'

EXPLORING THE ROLE – FESTIVAL ORGANISER

If the job of music director appealed to you and inspired your taste of being an organisational whiz, consider the open-air music festival!

There are summer festivals from rock festivals to the Notting Hill Carnival to legendary European open-air weekenders. (My brother, who lives in Spain, says that festivals there have the same kind of line-up as Glastonbury and the other big-name events here in the UK but without the obligatory rain and glorious mud.) Last year the famous Berlin Love Parade, which was 15 years old, attracted Pete Tong, Felix da Housecat and Paul van Dyk. Glastonbury ticket-sales cause panic every year and seem to sell out between sun-up and sundown.

- efestivals is a site that covers a good abundance of UK festivals (www.efestivals.co.uk/)

- www.glastonburyfestivals.co.uk/

- www.loveparade.de

- www.larmertree.co.uk

The Larmer Tree Festival is my favourite. Peacocks sit in the trees adding majesty to the scene and add their own brand of back-up singing to the stage acts.

'Spend the day lazing on the lawns against a backdrop of lush gardens with eastern temples and pagodas, paraded by iridescent peacocks. Soak up the unique atmosphere and quality music . . . when the sun sets and the lights illuminate the scene, get ready to dance the night away!

'Over 50 bands on five stages, including the return of the Acoustic Roots Cafe stage so bring an instrument! Camping is free for all ticket holders on a superb site right next to the festival. A perfect location with panoramic views, well equipped with free showers and ample well serviced toilet facilities.

'There are loads of free activities to keep the kids entertained – over 75 workshops, events and storytelling sessions culminating in the huge carnival procession around the gardens on Sunday afternoon.'

Source: www.larmertree.co.uk

I spoke to Co-Director, Julia Safe:

What kind of lifestyle does a festival organiser have? Is it one you recommend?
My festival is in July, so I would say my lifestyle is very seasonal – we work very hard from December through to August, and then take things a little easier in between. However it never stops; once the festival finishes, we immediately begin organising the next year.

I enjoy the lifestyle, the slow build up, the pressure of the impending deadline, followed by the relief and a good rest! It is definitely not 9 to 5, and every day is different.

Qualifications?
It is important to see as much new music as possible so it involves quite a lot of travelling to gigs. I live pretty much in the

middle of nowhere, so have to travel quite some distance to catch good music. I am also involved with programming the workshops and street theatre for the Larmer Tree Festival so make an annual pilgrimage to the Edinburgh Festival in August to keep up to date with new performers.

Also, I try to visit as many other festivals as possible over the summer, both to see new artists and keep an eye on the competition!

How do you start on a career as a festival organiser?
I started in a voluntary capacity, in the first year applying for funding from the local authority (managed to get £250 – it was 1993!), selling advertising for the programme and selling T-shirts and running the information desk at the actual festival.

All festivals have teams of volunteers who get involved with tasks like stewarding and backstage work, so this would be a good place to start. For the past eight years we have taken a student on placement from the BA (Hons) Arts and Event Production degree course at the Arts Institute at Bournemouth; they do a six-week placement as part of their second year; this gives them an excellent insight into the workings of our festival. Many of them now return to work for us at the weekend of the Festival and we have one ex-student currently with us on a six-month contract.

We are always very interested in volunteers who have worked at other events or festivals, so spending the summer volunteering at as many events as possible would be a very good start. The more experience you have, the more likely you will be to get an interesting volunteer role; you may have to start off with basic stewarding, and hopefully progress to the more interesting stuff.

So, where should a beginner start? Do you start with money/backing/sponsorship?
I would highly recommend a course in arts and events administration. They have many live projects; it is not just about being lectured at. This would give you the experience of planning, gaining sponsorship and funding for an event, and then most importantly seeing it through.

There is often funding available for new projects, but some kind of background, proven record, is usually required. Carefully targeting a potential sponsor may be successful, but again they are going to want to see proof that you can deliver.

I became involved with the Larmer Tree Festival in its third year, and my business partner James Shepard basically funded the first three years. We only began to break even in the fourth year, and then for several more years both continued to do other jobs as well as organising the festival in order to pay our rent. The growth of our festival has been slow and sure. It is very difficult to go in and make it work financially straight away.

How long does it take to organise a long-weekend festival like yours?

It is basically three single night concerts and then three full days. As I said earlier this takes all year to organise, there are two of us full-time and a production assistant is joining us for the six crucial months prior to the festival. This may sound like a long time for just about a week, but there is so much detail that goes into making it run as smoothly as possible.

What jobs do you start with and how far in advance of the first concert?

The first jobs are confirming the dates with the owners of the gardens that we hire for the festival, and also negotiating the fee and terms and conditions. The next crucial job is to start researching and booking headline acts; these things happen pretty much as soon as the previous festival has finished.

What permission do you need from the council, the parks, the police . . . Who else?

Even though the site that we use is private, we have to have a public entertainments licence from the local council. In fact we need two as our site straddles Wiltshire and Dorset. We have to do an extensive risk assessment, which is submitted with our application for the licence. This is checked by the local authority, police and fire brigade and we are in close communication with all of these bodies to ensure that the festival is safe for the audience.

Is there a career progression from concert organiser to venue music organiser to open-air music organiser?
Organising an open-air event is very different to organising a venue-based event, especially if, as in the case of the Larmer Tree, almost the entire infrastructure has to be put in, specifically stages, marquees, power, water and toilets. Programming the music is, although important, only part of organising a festival. Having a good knowledge of music, programming, marketing and dealing with musicians will of course be very useful skills to have in festival organisation.

What was your background before this?
I had a varied start, working in an antique business, publishing company, then secretarial temping all around London, followed by an arts foundation course, followed by a degree in three-dimensional design at Middlesex Polytechnic. Unfortunately on graduating I was struck down by repetitive strain injury which meant I was not able to work for some time. I moved away from London down to Wiltshire, and began volunteering at Salisbury Arts Centre, working on the box office and front of house. This is where I happened to be introduced to James and became involved with the festival. As I said previously, I worked at Salisbury Arts Centre (they gave me a job eventually!) for several more years before the Larmer Tree Festival was successful enough for it to be my sole income.

What are the pitfalls of being a festival organiser?
The stress and strain when a major headliner threatens to pull out (eventually it was resolved). It is a big responsibility to have the welfare of 4,000 people on your shoulders. The timing of the festival means that we are busiest just when the weather is starting to get good, so sometimes it feels like my summer doesn't start until the end of July. There are also sleepless nights worrying about 101 minor but crucial details.

What are the best moments?
Walking around the festival on Saturday afternoon when all of the glitches seem to have been solved, just observing all of these people having a brilliant time because of my last year's worth of work. That is very rewarding! Also, when it's all over and the feeling of relief and satisfaction after a successful festival is just

bliss. We get hundreds of emails from people telling us what a fantastic time they had, that it was the highlight of their year – this makes you feel pretty good.

What do you recommend about your work?
I love the creativeness of it, for example, booking the bands and other performers through to thinking about the decoration of the site, making sure that the 200 or so volunteers know what they are meant to doing and have a rewarding experience, and choosing fantastic food concessions.

How do I get started?
Just get involved with any festival or local event that you are interested in; see above regarding volunteering. Also consider volunteering at venues. Also courses as above. Offer your services to your local music promoter – putting up posters, handing out fliers at gigs, helping to write press releases, learn to use design software such as Photoshop so that you can design fliers, posters, offer to take money at the door . . .

What are the best qualities of a work experience person?
Preferably they will have some experience, however small, but also a positive attitude and determination to become involved (without pestering!) will usually be successful.

Transferable skill alert

By the way, there are also literary and arts festivals all over the place. If you're thinking of living up a musical life at university but plan to take, for example, a publishing career, think about the options. Think about transferable skills, what you can get involved in at university and how this might translate into the world of work. Think about what you'll be able to offer an employer.

If you want a career in the classical, jazz or blues areas, there are areas where knowledge gleaned here in this book can be applied.

Think about the process of recording and selling music. A piece of music needs to be targeted at an audience, for example. A CD needs production. A finished product needs a marketing strategy. Festival management applies to all genres and Julia Safe's advice (page 62) will stand you in good stead.

There are jobs that can be found in all music sectors: classical musicians need agents and artist management; music journalism covers all fields; orchestras and opera houses need press, publicity and marketing.

What about working for a broadcasting company? Radio stations and music TV channels need producers, presenters and studio managers. In live music transmission studio managers are often referred to as 'balancers' and are responsible for the sound of the orchestra.

If teaching is your vocation, check out Music Teachers UK (www.musicteachers.co.uk). It's a great resource! On their web page I found a wonderful interview/career profile by the composer Anwen Lewis in *Online Journal* (www.musicteachers.co.uk/journal).

Anwen Lewis is a freelance composer and coordinator for the School of Composition and Contemporary Music at the Royal Northern College of Music. She's also their Music Animateur, which means that she develops external education projects between the college and the community at large. Here's what she said when asked about the most exciting aspect of her professional life.

'On the education side of things, seeing the eyes of the people I work with open when they discover what they can do – that's not just the participants, but everybody who is involved.'

Orchestras, opera houses and radio stations often have 'outreach' departments or education departments. The staff of these departments get involved with schools and community groups. Music therapy is a branch of teaching and you can study this at many institutions. This is how the University of Bristol describes its Diploma in Music Therapy:

The course will equip musicians with the clinical, theoretical and practical skills required to enter the music therapy profession. The course complies with the standards and requirements for postgraduate music therapy training itemised by the Association of Professional Music Therapists and is validated by the Arts Therapists Board of the National Council of Professions Supplementary to Medicine. Graduates of the course are able to register with the APMT and to work within the existing career and grading structure as part of the National Health Service, within education, social services, the voluntary sector and privately. This part-time course enables mature students to continue in paid employment while studying.

Source: University of Bristol

If arts funding appeals to you take a look at the website of the Arts Council at www.artscouncil.org.uk. Also look at the 'Music' page of the British Council website:

From club-based DJ and VJ initiatives to jazz and traditional and folk to classical, we cover all genres of music. The Music Team in London works with our overseas network of arts managers and partners to plan, resource, deliver and evaluate high-impact arts projects involving professional artists and organisations from the UK. We aim to promote new images of Britain, to establish long-term partnerships abroad, and to attract young audiences. We also have our own weekly radio show *The Selector* featuring the best new music from the UK.

Source: www.britishcouncil.org

Orchestral management, or managing opera companies, choirs or ensembles, may fall under the category of running building-based organisations as defined by Leicester's De Montfort University. Their Arts Management course prepares you, they say, to be an orchestral manager or manager of a rock band, and presumably anything in between.

The degree prepares you for employment in a broad range of contexts from running theatres, arts centres and other building-based organisations to directly working with artists in dance, film production, theatre or music.

Alternatively you may wish to pursue a policy and community development pathway through the degree with a view to working in a public sector policy-making organisation such as a local authority, in community arts or public art.

Recent graduates have found employment in local radio, local authorities, festivals management, repertory theatres, the music industry, arts centres and in marketing.

Source: www.dmu.ac.uk

LASTLY, LET'S HEAD FOR HOLLYWOOD!

If you want to work in music for the film industry then look at the British Film Industry (BFI) website (www.britfilmusa.com/d_film_music.php).

Over 30% of Hollywood film scores alone are now recorded in the UK, and London is second only to LA in terms of the number of music soundtrack recordings it produces.
Source: www.britfilmusa.com/d_film_music.php

The site then boasts about UK recording facilities, our musicians and orchestras, composers, recording sessions and cost efficiency, not forgetting our music contractors, music producers, supervisors and copyright consultants. Take a look at the way they present these sectors to see if this is where your career path will take you.

There's plenty of scope for you to think about your 'transferable skills' as you make your way through this book and, as you enter the industry and make your way into your first and second jobs, keep considering your transferable skills and what you can offer a new sector with information gleaned from your last. It's a changing industry. Try to stay ahead and make your moves before you get pushed.

OTHER JOBS

Take a look at the music periodicals all of which have jobs pages. Make sure you get into the habit of looking at jobs pages and keep yourself in tune with the options available in this industry. For the sake of giving you a broad and bewildering idea of the amount and variation of jobs in the music industry I looked at *Music Week* (www.musicweek.com/jobs). Here's what I found. (Very few give salary details.)

ASSISTANT ENGINEER
Angel Recording Studios requires Assistant Engineer. Must have Pro Tools experience.

CAN YOU SELL MIDEM?
If you have several years' sales experience, are interested in Music and understand the changes and challenges facing the industry then this could be the job for you. We are the UK organisers of MIDEM, the world's leading International Music Exhibition where around 9,000 Industry professionals from all over the world gather in Cannes once a year to do business. You will be responsible for selling stands, participations, advertising and sponsorship at this important event. Apart from being a sales professional you will be well organised, used to dealing with clients at all levels, full of creative ideas and looking for a real career opportunity. We will pay the right salary for the right person.

EXP. ADMIN. PA
PA wanted to work with MD of busy independent music pub. co. Gen. admin., prep. contracts, song registration, copyright enquiries etc. A demanding job for someone with good tel. manner, exc. admin & comp. skills and ability to cope under pressure. Knowledge of royalties beneficial.

DIRECTOR OF INTERNATIONAL SALES AND MARKETING

Record company seeks the right individual to coordinate all international sales, marketing and promotional activities for their product line. The creation, implementation and overseeing of sales and marketing plans, relationship maintenance with our international distribution partners; coordination of advertising, press, touring, video and radio play in unison with our foreign promotion partners. Candidate must have a true grasp of the international music market along with proven sales experience.

AUDIO PRODUCT MANAGER

A rare and exciting opportunity exists to join our Music Buying Team. You must have previous similar buying experience, in-depth product knowledge, particularly of indie/alternative/leftfield music and singles. Existing relationships with suppliers and knowledge of import/export/one-stop markets would be an advantage. Excellent communication skills, self-motivation, tenacity and a methodical approach are essential to this role.

PA – VP £30K

High profile role providing seamless support to a senior international executive. Professional, confidential, diplomatic with unquestionable secretarial skills.

DIRECT MARKETING MANAGER

To develop and deliver ongoing e-business opportunities and commercially exploit the brand (major ent venue) through the application of technology and e-commerce.

LEGAL PA

A legal role with a twist. Hugely varied position for an accomplished legal secretary to support Legal Executive and the President within this major entertainment group.

INTERNET WEB DESIGNER (www.zeusrecords.com)

- Has real design flair and a creative eye for exciting web design

- Has a deep technical knowledge of all modern aspects of web design including COGI web scripting, Java, Macromedia Flash and competing technologies

- Has experience of designing and coding online shopping sites

- Innovative ideas about Internet music marketing and download purchasing

- Experience in collecting demographic online consumer information and converting that into increased online sales

- A passion in particular for electronica/dance, plus classical and film music

- Great interpersonal skills

- A willingness to expand skills, enjoy working in a high-tech atmosphere and work flexibly to ensure deadlines are met

- Able to work from home

STORE MANAGER
You must have at least 2 years' retail management experience with a comprehensive knowledge of our industry. Strong customer service skills, a keen eye for detail and a practical hands-on approach to store operations is imperative.

LABEL MANAGER
Responsibilities include devising concepts, planning release schedules, monitoring budgets, liaising with licensors and compilers, design, repro and print companies and co-ordinating marketing and PR across a number of Union Square's key labels.

ROYALTIES SUPERVISOR £25K

You will need 3 years' recent royalties experience ideally within a label or collection society with supervisory experience for this indie.

ARTISTS ROYALTIES SUPERVISOR £25K

Managing work delegation, training, development and recruitment. You will also assist the Royalties Director in systems improvement and testing, and relationship building and strengthening both internally and externally. Extensive artist royalties experience is essential – ideally at a supervisory level.

AUDIO ROYALTIES CONTROLLER £22K

Responsibilities include ensuring contractual obligations to international contributors are managed and guidance is given to junior Administrators. You will also present information to Finance Managers and other departments on a regular basis, and produce statements for Independent Producers. Candidates must have at least 18 months' royalties experience.

PRESS OFFICER (www.cmoves.co.uk)

Major Record Label require a Press Officer with 2 years' experience in a similar role with a specialist interest in Rock and Indie. The ideal candidate will possess skills necessary to establish strong working relationships with journalists, artists, artist managers and product managers. Main duties will also include coordinating foreign press trips, composing press releases and providing creative input for artists' photo shoots.

CHAPTER 6

Brave new world

Where are the new jobs? What are the implications of cheap computer software and electronically equipped teenagers? What about the changing nature of music ownership and publishing rights? Where are the opportunities in the new era of Internet and music downloading and the changing nature of music sales and record company revenues? This 'brave new world' is also changing the nature of music 'outlets' – taking away the power that the radio DJ used to wield. It's full of moving targets, which spreads confusion. There are optimists and pessimists on this subject.

I spoke to Jez Broster, former A&R Manager at Randor Music London and A&R consultant for Sony/Columbia Records. He was also an artist manager. He has now moved into radio production and moved out of the industry. He complains that entrepreneurs and interesting characters are being squeezed out and the serious suits are staying in. He also points out that media outlets for music that is 'slightly different' are disappearing. No one wants to champion those types of artists. He argues that the major companies are not geared for innovative sorts of music.

I asked him to explain further. I argued that creative, innovative, entrepreneurial types can't be kept down and kept quiet. I argued that if traditional backrooms of pubs are lost as venues for new bands then bands will find other places – I've heard of churches being used. And, laws or no laws, people will always dance. If independent record labels have been swallowed up by the big boys, independence will flower elsewhere, surely!

Jez argued back. See what you think about his argument. Many people are leaving the industry having come to exactly the same conclusions as Jez.

SHRINKING VIOLET?

'Consider the shrinking industry. All of these small record companies, employing 40 or so people, representing their own brand of music are now just one company, Universal: A&M, Polydor, MCA, Island, Defjam, Interscope, London, Mercury, Phonogram and Fontana.

'Sony UK has swallowed up Columbia, Epic and S2 and seems about to merge with BMG. BMG itself has already consumed RCA and Arista.

'Warner Bros bought out WEA, Atlantic, Electra, Warner Bros and East West. EMI is now EMI/Virgin. EMI might merge with Warner or be bought by Edger Brothman (Seegrams) so even the big boys are being absorbed.

'Stand alones and small concerns are gone. East West might have had 80 bands in the Eighties on which they are spending studio and promotion money and hoping to break through with a big money spinner. This is called the unrecouped artist – they have yet to prove themselves financially. Today Sony UK might have seven or eight unrecouped artists. This means that a new S Club or Westlife are worth signing but most new bands lose money hand over fist. Back catalogues like that belonging to Bruce Springsteen, for example, can be repackaged and reintroduced to the next generation and have endless money-making potential.'

Since I met Jez for this discussion more and more changes have taken place. All of this is incredibly interesting, not to say heartbreaking for those of us who remember the Eighties heyday. What about the Sixties when the record company really meant something? Consider Motown or Stax or Trojan. What about the punk era and Stiff Records?

For an extensive list of record labels take a look at 'Wikipedia' (http://en.wikipedia.org/wiki/List_of_record_labels). It's the Internet encyclopaedia. This page also states that, as of 2003, the five global giants in the music and entertainment industry control 70–80% of the worldwide music output, backing up Jez's pessimism.

RIDE THE WAVES OF CHANGE

Yet if you look at the Wikipedia webpage describing 'record labels', there is a small section on 'The emergence of open-source labels'. Their definition states:

'The new century brings the phenomena of the open-source or open-content record label. These are inspired by the free software and open-source movement and the success of GNU/Linux.'

Source: Wikipedia

The example they give is LOCA Records. Wikipedia gives a link to the LOCA home page. Take a look and see what you think.

Here's another thing that is shaking up the music industry, taking the money from its old home and putting it in a new pocket – 'music masters ownership'. What does this mean? Jez has more to contribute to his thesis that the music industry is dying:

'In the traditional world of making records and signing someone, most record companies want finished masters before signing. (All copies emanate from the one, original 'master'.) Artists are now producing their professional-quality masters at home so the legal ownership of the master does not necessarily belong to the company. So what happens to the way a record company earns its money if they don't have ownership of the physical recording?

'Therefore, there's the traditional chain of ownership versus the new/potential claim which bypasses the status quo.'

Well, Jez and I could have argued for ever. In his opinion, the music industry is dying. I hear those very words from other sources and see it in headlines and I wonder what they are talking about.

My conclusion is that you will have to read about and ride all of these changes; be prepared for them, clue yourself up with as much of the technological skills as you need, as many of the short courses as will spur you on, as many contacts as you can fit into a contact book, as many qualifications as you think will make you indispensable, and, more than anything, be prepared for the knocks and the long haul.

In this book, I've asked many of the contributors to talk about their use of new technology and the new musical age and I've given you the sparkling profile of a man stuffed to the eyeballs with qualifications, experience, who is also unanimously loved by colleagues . . . and made redundant. Have some savvy. Then be a star!

CHAPTER 7

Start off with study

'there are now in excess of 500 different possible courses at over 200 establishments'
Source: British Phonographic Industry
Music Education Directory

This book represents people who have had an academic education up to degree level, those who have acquired their skills through schemes, community centres and evening classes, and those who are fully self-taught and rely on learning from those in the industry. Let's recap:

- Andrea Terrano featured on page 30 has his own studio and studied sound engineering and became a teacher and took short courses wherever possible.

- Moshik featured on page 15 decided against formal education in his career choices to be a sound engineer and musician/composer.

- Neil Gardener on page 26 is a teacher at the Gateway School of Recording and Music Technology and says training is essential for a career as a sound engineer.

- In Chapter 4, 'Where do you fit in?' Alice Schofield of Anglo Plugging doesn't assume any formal qualifications for people wanting work experience but plenty of office skills and a confident manner are essential.

- Sam Elderidge is the manager of the band Ludes, featured on page 40. He studied English Literature at degree level. He made full use of his time out of the lecture room to pursue his music career.

- Ahmad Dayes, the producer featured in Chapter 5, 'Job Profiles', found that, after A-levels, the Midi Music Company offered the practical training he needed. Ahmad discovered that MMC was fully equipped with industry-standard equipment, that classes were taught by people still working in the industry, and that contacts offered by the centre ensured ready and supported access to work placements and jobs.

- Oliver X who features on page 48 took a BSc in European Business and Technology and a Master's degree in Sales and Marketing.

- DJ NIKKI has a Fine Art degree and is classically trained in piano and cello. She also recommends a 'business mentality'.

- Laure Malca featured on page 58 as a director of music for a World Music venue has a Master's degree in Contemporary History.

- Julia Safe is a Festival Organiser and recommends a BA (Hons) Arts and Event Production degree. She has a degree in three-dimensional design at Middlesex Polytechnic.

Once again I'll point you in the direction of the *Music Education Directory* produced by the BPI (www.bpi-med.co.uk) to find the right course for you, from evening classes to postgraduate qualifications. They say that 'there are now in excess of

500 different possible courses at over 200 establishments'. The layout of the directory splits courses up into sections and subsections: Business/Sociology, Creative/instrumental, and Tech/Audio Engineering. Then they list the recommended a) degree courses, b) college courses and c) training.

They then use an example of a course and point out the various levels of information. To illustrate, they use the BA (Hons) in Performance Arts: Music or Community Music, Diploma in Popular Music and Sound Technology.

They give a description of the course, which in this case covers performance, composition, teaching, arts and education administration. They give the length of the course and number of student places available. Next are the application details, interview time and audition and enrolment dates and procedures. Then entry requirements (this one in Liverpool doesn't have particular entry requirements but 'factors considered'). There are, of course, student funding details, work placement opportunities and indication of industry professionals teaching on the course and well as contact details.

There really is everything you need to get an idea of the range of courses available, the variety of qualifications required, and the *Directory* should be read in order to get a grasp of the array of skills that the music industry is looking for. For more information on this directory see page 82.

In your interview for a course you must prove that it was a considered choice. Prove that you thought about the course content, the reputation of the institution, the track record of the teachers, the employment outcomes of the graduates (the department will hold statistics), the contacts with the industry and the placements possible.

Here are a couple of examples of graduate employment details you can find:

The University of Salford BA Hons in Acoustics has a graduate employment record that they describe thus:

'Salford Acoustics graduates have an excellent employment record. Previous graduates have obtained employment with companies like Philips (Holland), Bang and Olufsen (Denmark), Sandy Brown Associates and Hepworth Acoustics.'

The University of Westminster refurbished its studio facilities with huge investment and their course in Music Business Management: 'aims to prepare you to be an agent of change in the music industry.'

Cliché warning:
To invest in yourself costs money but not to invest in yourself costs more.

Please be aware of the Youth Music Action Zones, which are active in 'some of Britain's most disadvantaged areas'. It's a national charity to help people up to 18 years of age to make music. It aims, by 2006, to have involved more than one million children and young people in its music making opportunities. The National Lottery and Arts Council of England are among its sources of funding. There's a website, www.youthmusic.org.uk/Action_Zones.jsp, which profiles various jobs in the industry but there's a lot more than that on offer.

Here are a few of the projects around the country and an example of things they do – it's a tiny taster:

Sound Futures in Birmingham stages DJ and sound production lessons.
Remix in Bristol and Gloucester had Courtney Pine conduct workshops.
Gmmaz in Manchester set up a recording studio.
Music4u in Humber runs percussion projects.
Sound Connections in London hosts music business seminars.
Mzone in Liverpool runs a drumming programme.
                          Check it out: www.youthmusic.org.uk

Visit the 'news page' on the Youth Music website. Here are a couple of things I found:

'WANTED: Young musicians from Hampshire to perform live at Homelands!'

'Humber Action Zone launches Latin American and African drumming project.'

LOOK IT UP
Youth Music Action Zones
1 America Street, London SE1 0NE
Tel: 020 7902 1060
www.youthmusic.org.uk

'Hip Hop legends Arrested Development, The Spooks and Lifesavas support DONATE-A-DATE.'

Other lists of courses
The BPI's *Music Education Directory* really does have everything you need to know about courses. It can be ordered from the BPI Education department at a cost of £5. Email: education@bpi.co.uk. The directory is produced by BPI Education and sponsored by the PRS, the MCPS, British Music Rights, PPL, the Musicians' Union, the IRMA and the Federation of Music Collectives (see Contacts pages) and all of them have pooled their advice to applicants which includes, for example, what questions you need to ask yourself about the course facilities and links with the industry which will help you gain access after your studies.

The BPI also produces a *Directory of BPI Members* from which you can get record company descriptions and details so you can start writing off for your work experience placements.

Their website is very detailed. The careers pages have sections on: 'Careers and Education'; 'The Brit School'; 'Access All Areas'; 'Training Courses'; 'the Music Education Directory' (online); and 'Useful Resources'.

On the Connexions website (www.connexions.gov.uk) there are a couple of articles there that might be of interest to you. A bit of investigation will show which ones are for musicians and which for management.

Make use of your library and the websites I've mentioned. Also, make use of careers guidance in your school or college.

Enjoy the BBC website (www.bbc.co.uk/radio1/onemusic/guides) which offers information about getting into the music industry.

'www.hotcourses.com provides the largest and most accurate course database available. We do not restrict ourselves to one particular sector of education, so you can find undergraduate and postgraduate degrees, leisure courses and professional development courses all on the same site. Hotcourses also appears on learndirect.co.uk.'

If you do decide to go to university or spend time in further education, spend some of your spare time productively. If music is your passion you don't need me to tell you that! It really doesn't matter what you choose to study as long as you are following a real interest and not studying to be a doctor just to please the parents! There are plenty of ways of building up experience while you're in further or higher education that will contribute towards a sparkling CV. Take a look at the choices Sam Elderidge made. (See Chapter 5, 'Job Profiles'.)

Sam wanted to pursue his interest in English literature as well as enter the music business and so went to university. Sam says that there is no snobbery associated with the industry in terms of education. It is a very tolerant and inclusive environment as long as you approach it with the same attitude. However, he spent his non-literary time actively building up his CV and making contacts. Here's how:

'I wrote for student papers, the BBC in the North East and had a student radio show. Which were all really instrumental in building up my CV for the music business. Most major record companies also have student reps and this is a great way to actively become involved with a company outside of just work experience. All the above uni activities were key, plus I had done a lot of work experience at ad agencies that dealt with Sony, and at Virgin Books writing on the best music stores in London.'

Well, university does all the usual things such as offer the first steps to leaving home, the first experience of independence and finding your vocation in life but, given that funding is such a sharp concern, you'll be wondering if a degree is the best route into the biz. I hope this book has given you some clues and some alternatives. At least you're well armed to quiz your careers teacher at school now.

LIVING THE DREAM

When you're up against it, banging your head against a brick wall, think about Jentina who is enjoying a brilliant record-signing deal with Virgin and the imminent release of her first single and an album release by Christmas.

Her story is a unique one, with a lot of struggle, tough times and hustling, bags of nerve and tons of ambition. She has a spirit of adventure and cracking amount of tenacity. I admire her more than most people I know who are double her age.

Jentina had a problematic upbringing, with plenty of run-ins with the law, and at the age of 13 her mother chucked her out. A dinner lady from school gave her a home and it's with her sons that Jentina learnt to rap and MC. She tried being a Garage MC one night and that was it. She went back every Saturday night.

At 15 years of age she bought a ticket to Miami and lived off her wits out there until she was deported back to the UK. From there she got a job in a Soho gallery and hustled for everything.

A friend lent her a laptop with a music program on it. She started putting down her thoughts and creativity. The same friend told her to get in touch with a producer friend but she didn't bother. The friend persisted, though, and arranged for the producer to visit the gallery and hear her stuff.

'From nothing, somebody believed in me.'

From then (17–19 years old) she almost lived in his studio and wrote and recorded, on the smallest amount of money and the largest amount of borrowing.

And so we arrive at today with a fully crafted collection of tracks to exchange for a single and album deal with Virgin.

Now that she's living her dream, how does she reflect on the path she's taken? She says it was all over in a second! And her advice? She says, 'Carry yourself and believe in yourself and everyone around you will believe in you.'

So when you think you've had enough and you'll get an ordinary job in an ordinary town think about Jentina's reason for keeping going. She says, 'It's not like following a dream but being attached to a string and being pulled.'

The last time I spoke to Jentina she was waiting for her choreographer to be flown over from Los Angeles!

And, finally, she's dancing all the way to the bank.

Hope you do too.

CONTACTS

Access To Music
18 York Road
Leicester LE1 5TS
Tel: 0800 281842
Website: www.access-to-music.co.uk

British Music Rights (BMR)
British Music House
26 Berners Street
London W1P 3DB
Tel: 020 7306 4446
Website: www.bmr.org

British Phonographic Society (BPI)
R25 Savile Row
London W1X 1AA
Tel: 020 7851 4000
(*Music Education Directory* and careers advice)
Website: www.bpi.co.uk

Fat Cat website
www.fat-cat.co.uk/diy
This is designed to help new artists find out what they need to
know to get their own work out into the world.

Federation of Music Collectives (FMC)
Space 28
North Lotts
Dublin 1
Ireland
Tel: +353 1 8782244
Website: www.fmc-ireland.com

International Federation of Phonographic Industries (IFPI)
5th Floor
54–62 Regent Street
London W1B 5ER
Tel: 020 7878 7900
Website: www.ifpi.org

International Recording Media Association (IRMA)
182 Nassau Street, Suite 204
Princeton
New Jersey 08542
USA
Tel: +1 609 279 1700
Website: www.recordingmedia.org

Mechanical Copyright Protection Society (MCPS)
Elgar House
41 Streatham High Road
London SW16 1ER
Tel: 020 8769 4400
Website: www.mcps.co.uk

Musicians' Union
National Office
60–62 Clapham Road
London SW9 0JJ
Tel: 020 7582 5566
Website: www.musiciansunion.org.uk

Music Publishers Association (MPA)
3rd Floor Strandgate
18/20 York Buildings
London WC2N 6JU
Tel: 020 7839 7779
Website: www.mpaonline.co.uk

Phonographic Performance Limited (PPL)
1 Upper James Street
London W1F 9DE
Tel: 020 7534 1000
Website: www.ppluk.com

Performing Rights Society (PRS)
Copyright House
29–33 Berners Street
London W1T 3AB
Tel: 020 7580 5544
Website: www.prs.co.uk